LIFE OF
THE PARTY

LIFE OF THE PARTY

A Political Press Tart Bares All

Lisa Baron

CITADEL PRESS
Kensington Publishing Corp.
www.kensingtonbooks.com

CITADEL PRESS BOOKS are published by

Kensington Publishing Corp.
119 West 40th Street
New York, NY 10018

All Kensington titles, imprints, and distributed lines are available at special quantity discounts for bulk purchases for sales promotions, premiums, fundraising, educational, or institutional use. Special book excerpts or customized printings can also be created to fit specific needs. For details, write or phone the office of the Kensington special sales manager: Kensington Publishing Corp., 119 West 40th Street, New York, NY 10018, attn: Special Sales Department; phone 1-800-221-2647.

CITADEL PRESS and the Citadel logo are Reg. U.S. Pat. & TM Off.

First printing: July 2011

10 9 8 7 6 5 4 3 2 1

Printed in the United States of America

CIP data is available.

ISBN-13: 978-0-8065-3415-2
ISBN-10: 0-8065-3415-X

TO: Marilyn, Joe, Michael, and Micah

This book is written in memory of Elizabeth "Lizzie" Prostic, who was taken by breast cancer way too soon into her young life. Lizzie was the coolest, smartest, and most beautiful woman to ever walk the halls of congress. A woman who never relied on anyone to get her anywhere she wanted to be.

A percentage of the proceeds from this book will go to the Michael Steven Schwartz Education Scholarship Fund. Please buy two copies. My agent gets a percentage too.

Contents

Contents

Author's Note

If you are a friend or relative of my mother, this book may or may not be true. Please make a note of this.

To everyone else: This book is a compilation of events that took place in my life during the years 1999–2006ish. At least that's my memory of it. Some of the characters' names have been changed because this book should make everyone laugh, not cry or be the cause of loss of employment. Timelines have been compressed or slightly altered to adhere to a swift and easy storytelling process in fewer than a thousand pages. This ain't no *War and Peace*, bitches!

LIFE OF
THE PARTY

Red, White, and Booze

Remember the first politician you voted for? The one whose fiery speeches and slick, visionary campaign commercials drove you to the polls? You wanted to record your vote for someone you believed in and to come back from your lunch break with one of those little round stickers that reads, "I voted."

Or maybe it was that soul-shaking stump speech from a presidential nominee who was so powerful, so moving, it had you pumping your fists, jumping on your couch shouting "YES WE CAN! YES, WE CAN!" You didn't just feel it—you believed it. Maybe you mustered the courage to do something that just the day before yesterday intimidated you.

We, the twentysomething staffers who actually write the stump speeches, produce the campaign commercials, and dictate the overall tone of a campaign, appreciate your enthusiasm. We are happy to have made a difference in your life; it's what we live for. It's what gets us up at

5 A.M. and keeps us awake until 2 A.M. But we have lives of our own that also need some tending to.

Take Jon Favreau, President Obama's twenty-nine-year-old White House speech director. After putting back a few dozen brewskis at a holiday party (post-election), he went to second base with a life-size cardboard cutout of Hilary Clinton. He got into trouble when the pictures surfaced on his Facebook page. Not only did he have to take down the pictures, he was forced to apologize to the future secretary of state for pretending to grab her boob. As funny as it is, I feel for Jon. I've been to parties where there were twenty-seven-year-old boys, and I can tell you this is what they do after a few beers: they dry-hump cardboard cutouts of famous people.

Favreau is not the first youngster to ride around in Air Force One wearing a pair of trendy Ray-Ban Aviators and designer jeans. A study recently published in the *Washington Post* shows that the average age of a staffer on the Hill, including those involved with writing legislation, is about twenty-five. That's right; and the average age skews slightly younger for campaign and political committee staff. Sometimes these kids have staffs of their own.

Louisiana Governor Bobby Jindal, born June 10, 1971 (one year before I was born), is the youngest current governor in the United States. Before he was elected governor, he was a two-term congressman, and before that, he was appointed secretary of the Louisiana Department of Health and Hospitals (DHH), and before that, well, you get the picture—Jindal started kicking some governmental ass at a very young age.

While some young people are running the world, others are ruining it. If you live in DC, it's quite possible that the girl or boy who sat next to you at your favorite watering hole this past weekend—you know, the loud one who was slamming Jaegermeister?—probably wrote the legislation that deregulated Wall Street and as a result, shook the international financial system to its very core.

This begs the question: Who are these kids running our country, and why do they have so much power?

We are tenacious, ambitious, and qualified to work eighteen-hour days. We have healthy hearts built to endure the immense stress on little sleep and junk food. We can work the people's business like it's nobody's business, because we have a high tolerance for alcohol and enough brain cells still left to function through a hangover. But we also have another asset—we're a blank slate. We haven't been tarnished by old campaigns or old grudges. But after the first high-profile campaign you are a part of that loses, you'd better count on sitting the next few election cycles out. The next elected official you go to sign up with will assume that it was you who was calling the shots that caused the campaign to bomb. Sometimes the young ones take the bullet for the senior shot callers.

Consider the story of former White House political director Sara Taylor. She was in her twenties when she went to work in the White House Political Office at the discretion of Karl Rove. At thirty she was appointed political director. Two years later she was embroiled in scandal. That's right: a thirty-two-year-old—a finance major from Iowa's Drake University, with no formal legal background—was messing with the United States judicial system, participating in the firing of U.S. attorneys and then trying to appoint new ones. Of course, she was being told what to do by someone else, but that somebody else gave a thirty-two-year-old way more power than she should have had. That's kind of fucked up.

I spent my roaring twenties, and far too much of my thirties, as the confidant and right-hand woman to possibly the greatest grassroots organizer of all time: Ralph Reed, the former executive director of the

Christian Coalition. I began working with Ralph in the fall of 1999, when I was twenty-six years old and hell-bent on making it to the White House. I helped elect him Georgia State party chairman in 2001, created a platform for his state-wide office run, and was his spokeswoman in 2005, during the very public Abramoff lobbying scandal (recently depicted in the Kevin Spacey flick *Casino Jack,* with Neve Campbell's brother playing Ralph—go figure)—all while trying to have a life of my own. By the time it was done, I was overexposed, tarred by scandal, and had a whole new view of the Christian Coalition, politics, and my purpose in life. Looking back on the wild ride, though, I realize that I was part of a band of wild kids running our country, and I can't fathom why Americans aren't demanding that our leaders go through a sober process of apprenticeship before handing them the reins of power.

But what do I know? I'm just another press tart, trying to save the world, one hot guy at a time. This is my story.

CHAPTER 1

Holy Fuck

When people find out that I worked for Ralph Reed during the 2000 Republican presidential primary in South Carolina, they always ask the same thing: Was it true Ralph told voters that Senator John McCain fathered a black child? And my answer is always the same, "How would I know? I was in a Greenville hotel room giving Ari Fleischer a blow job."

Now oral sex, with anyone, particularly the aforementioned former George W. Bush White House press secretary, is typically not the sort of physical activity one brags about or broadcasts, or for that matter, inserts into the opening pages of her first book. In fact, some girls are loath to admit to hovering over a man's shaft for any extended period of time—an activity that, from an aerial view, looks like you're bobbing for apples, and losing.

So why then would I accept a one-eyed flesh monster during a road trip through the 2000 South Carolina presidential primary with the former director of the Christian Coalition, Ralph Reed? Because back in those days I was a fearless, frisky, and tenacious twenty-six-year-old press tart with starry eyes, a short skirt, and a passion for civics. To be able to say, "I'm with the such-and-such campaign" or I work for "Senator So-and-So" is to us political junkies what "I'm with the band" is to Pamela Des Barres. My remarkable encounter with Ari in that unremarkable hotel room perfectly summed up my groupie-like relationship to politics at that time—I wanted it, I worshipped it, and I went for it.

If you're not a news geek, you may not know about Ralph Reed. Ralph was the former executive director of the Christian Coalition, turned political presidential power broker. Under the tutelage of televangelist turned presidential candidate Pat Robertson, Ralph organized legions of religious conservative voters and formed a mega-Christian voting block that became an essential piece of any Republican candidate's trajectory for public office. At one point in history, Ralph was so powerful and ubiquitous that *Time* magazine devoted an entire edition to him. The cover of the magazine, dated May 15, 1995, featured a menacing picture of him under the banner headline, "The Right Hand of God."

Ralph's public persona is well documented: he is a Christian caped crusader ridding the world of profanity and porn. Smooth and charismatic, he could work a bank of cameras like George Clooney could work a small town waitress. When I started working for him, Ralph was a thirtysomething über-zealot with a hard drinking past, a taste for the good life, and a hunger for power. His movie-star good looks (Ralph, you're welcome) and uncanny ability to articulate conservative thoughts and policies into easily digestible sound bites made him a force to contend with. His baby face was the mug for a movement that cried out for decency, prayer, and moments of God in everyday life. It was Ralph Reed who, along with Dick Armey, Tom DeLay, and Newt Gingrich, wrested Congress from the party of Bill Clinton.

In 1998, Ralph left Washington, DC, and the Christian Coalition to move to Duluth, a northern suburb in Georgia, where he opened up Century Strategies, a private grassroots-lobbying firm. This is where I come in—he hired me, a twentysomething socially moderate Jew (yes, some Jewish girls do give blowjobs) to be his personal publicist. An unlikely partnership? Not as much as you'd think. I was the perfect mouthpiece for Ralph—an impeccably dressed sinner who could work the dirty but delicate business of press, while Ralph focused his Evangelical might on building a corporate empire.

In Ralph, I found the man who I thought could make my own political dreams come true, and in me, Ralph found the perfect minion. As long as we both held up each side of the bargain, it was a partnership made in heaven—no matter which Bible you thump. For six years, I accompanied Ralph on his various political missions, starting, stoking, and putting out fires wherever the need required. Some trips were more interesting than others.

Ari, whom you may also be unfamiliar with, was President George W. Bush's White House press secretary from 2000 to 2003. Notoriously tight-lipped and hostile to the press, he was at the helm during the September 11 attacks on the World Trade Center. I knew him before he had become the stoic and unflappable mouthpiece for the leader of the free world, the voice of the president (did someone say WMDs?) during one of the most controversial moments in modern political history. I had met him on the job a few years prior, in the romantic state of Iowa. It was caucus time, I was unemployed, and the head of the Iowa

Republican Party had called me and invited me to help out with press. Of course, I agreed—I was trying to set myself up for the next presidential campaign, and this represented a good networking opportunity.

All the Republicans in town were hanging out at a particular steak house—me included—and unbeknownst to me, a pre-Bush era Ari Fleischer had singled me out in the crowd. He asked a mutual friend of ours, a pollster called Tony, who I was. A couple of days later, Tony and I were talking and he casually recounted the conversation to me.

"Who's Ari?" I asked nonchalantly.

"Can I give him your number?" asked Tony, who was known in some circles as Tony the Rat.

I thought about it for a second. At the time, Ari was very important in political circles. He was working for Elizabeth Dole, and it was clear he was headed for great things.

"Okay. Give him my number."

Ari called and invited me to have dinner with him next time I was in DC. At the time, I was screwing around with the very dapper David Israelite, political director for the Republican National Committee. I really liked David, but he wasn't so into the whole girlfriend/boyfriend thing. So, what's a girl to do but move on to the next? It was not long after being told by David for the twentieth time that he didn't want a relationship that I announced "Okay, well, I'm going out with Ari." I found myself dining at the George Hotel restaurant with Mr. Fleischer soon after.

It would be marvelous if I could recall the details of what we ate, what I wore, the ambience, our wonderful conversation—but I can't. I was waist deep in martinis (extra olives). And as such, my memories are on the fuzzy side. You will notice that this is typical of my entire twenties. I do recall, however, that we went back to his town house apartment and got down and dirty like my martini. I think there might have been a porno involved, but I can't be sure. The next day, he drove me back to my hotel, and I wondered if he still wanted to date me. *I mean, who would want to be with a bad girl like me?* I thought, giggling to myself, and realizing—I didn't care one way or the other.

My next tryst with Ari took place in Atlanta, at my apartment. I had no chairs, no kitchen table, no couch—my monthly paycheck was always devoted to expanding my magnificent, some would say comprehensive, collection of Diane von Furstenberg cocktail dresses and Stuart Weitzman shoes. So, when Ari asked if he could come and stay with me (he had tickets to a baseball game in town), there really wasn't anywhere for him to sleep—except in my bed; I mean my mattress on the floor, with me. "Sure, why not?" I said. At the time, I was already working for Ralph Reed, and clearly, Ralph's saintly morals had yet to penetrate my press tart's armor. I went to the baseball game with Ari; we came home. At the time, I had no idea that that he was in negotiations to become George W. Bush's press secretary. Had I known, I probably would have screamed louder during the money shot.

He left town the next day, and soon after, got the job with George W. Bush, who had, coincidentally, tapped my boss, Ralph Reed, to rally the support of the religious right in his bid to become the Republican presidential nominee. The 2000 South Carolina primary would provide the backdrop for my third meeting with Ari. Tensions were running high in the two-horse race, between Bush and United States Senator John McCain (R-AZ). The primary war in the South had become civil, and when you pit brother against brother, things can get downright ugly. Rumors had begun to circulate about McCain's adopted child, suggesting that the kid was conceived Strom Thurmond–style: with a black woman. No one is sure where the rumors came from, and more than once, I've had to remind people that no, I don't know if it was Ralph who had planted the seed, because at the time I was busy helping Ari Fleischer spread his seed.

I'll just call Ari and see what he is doing, I thought, as soon as I arrived in Greenville, upstate South Carolina, for the primary. I was in my twenties and I thought it was pretty cool that I had George W. Bush's press secretary's number on my speed dial. (I'm not proud, just honest.) I had driven down there with Ralph, and Big Les, Ralph's fortysomething, ever loyal menopausal executive assistant. During the day, Ralph and I passed out George Bush literature and made friends with the locals at pancake-flipping contests. When he wasn't smiling and shaking hands, Ralph would be taking e-mails and calls from Karl Rove. And I'd be taking calls from Ari. Turns out, we were all staying in the same hotel. By further coincidence, Ari's room was right next to Ralph's.

"Come knock on my door when you get back," said Ari. As soon as I was sure that Ralph and his wife were in their room for the night, I tapped on Ari's door. I had had a cocktail or three—sometimes it's the only way to wind down after a long day on the campaign trail. Ari and I started kissing, and I felt giddy, giddy about the primary race, and high on the inappropriateness of the moment. I will say this—I was not keen on getting that room a-rocking, as I did not want Ralph or his wife to come a-knocking. As much as I knew politics could be a rough-and-tumble business, Ralph and his wife were right next door, and, well, Ralph had always been so good to me. Even though I didn't share his beliefs, I respected him, as an upholder of family values, as a brilliant speaker and academic, and as a boss I trusted to take my career where it needed to go.

Since audible sex was out of the question, I immediately headed south and took care of business. With each bob of my head, I considered my options.

"I won't sleep over," I said to myself as my head descended.

LIFE OF THE PARTY

"Okay, I will sleep over, but I'll leave before Ari wakes up," I said on the ascend.

"But I will leave while Ari is asleep," I promised on a more rapid decline.

When it was clear that my job was done (if you know what I mean and I think you know what I mean), I fell asleep and awoke as early as I had ever gotten up, around 5:30 A.M. only to find Ari already out of bed, scanning the day's newspapers to prepare himself and his candidate, the future president of the United States, for the day.

I was twenty seven, and Ari was forty. He was just one in a string of casual lovers of mine, the big difference being he also had the job I had dreamed of for so long—he was the White House press secretary. Après hummer, I tiptoed out into the hallway and made a dash for the room I was sharing with Big Les. I really hoped that Ralph didn't decide this would be a good time to take a stroll and catch me stumbling out of Ari's room, all red cheeks, bed head, and vodka breath. Even through my alcohol fog, I didn't want to let Ralph down.

CHAPTER 2

Tart, Interrupted

I was born Lisa Beth Schwartz in Los Angeles, California, second of three children to happily married Jewish parents. My mother, Marilyn, was a blond, petite, preschool teacher from the Midwest, a powerhouse whose diminutive stature belied her iron will. My father, Michael—tall, dark, and dashing—was my Superman. Funny, charismatic, and loved by all, if there had been Eskimos in LA, he would have been the one selling them ice.

We lived in the San Fernando Valley in a comfortable home in the suburban neighborhood of Canoga Park, neighbored by film producers, young families, and the occasional porn star. This being Los Angeles, showbiz regularly infiltrated everyday life—my older sister, Robyn, used to roller-skate with the late Dana Plato, the tragic child star who played Kimberly in *Diff'rent Strokes*, for example. I could have grown up a typical Jewish Valley Girl, saying things like "rad," convinced that Dweezil and Moonbeam were entirely appropriate names for offspring, but when I was six, my parents declared they had had enough of California, and moved us all—me, my sister Robyn and my baby brother, Scott—to our brand-new home in Arizona. My mom explained that the move was based on health issues, her really bad "allergies"—allergies, I learned, was another word for "mother-in-law." So we waved good-bye to the palm trees, the smog, and Dana Plato, and headed for the dry desert city of Phoenix.

We had been in Phoenix for just about a year when my father went on a business trip to Tennessee. My dad traveled often, and usually when he returned he would take us to Toys "R" Us where we each could pick out a toy. He would hold my mom's hand as we kids charged through the automatic sliding doors, I headed straight to the Barbie aisle, where I would have my new BFF picked out in under ten minutes. My big sister, on the other hand, lolly-gagged around the toy super store sometimes for two hours racking her brain, and my nerves, trying to pick her poison. But this time, he never came back from his business trip. There were three of them in the car when a drunk driver, being chased by the police after fleeing another accident, lost control of his vehicle, swerved over the median, and hit them head-on. I was seven years old.

Because I couldn't comprehend the notion of death, I conjured my own version of events—my dad was on an extended business trip, I told myself. Even after his funeral, I made myself believe that he was, in actual fact, traveling, as he so often did, and the reason he couldn't come home was because he had another family someplace else that he had to look after. He had chosen them over us. Meanwhile, my mother, newly widowed and a single parent to three children, did her best to shield us from the trauma of losing our father. She didn't skip a beat—even in the direct aftermath of my dad's death, it was business as usual. I didn't miss a ballet lesson, a horseback-riding lesson, or (unfortunately) a Hebrew class. I rarely saw her mourn—just once, I sat outside her bedroom door on the cold marble floor, listening to her reckon with God. Deep down, I knew that one day, I would have to accept that my dad, Michael, wasn't going to come back. But for most of my childhood, it was easier to believe that we were all playing a game of hide-and-seek, and that soon enough my dad would pop out from behind the sofa and yell, "Surprise!" and we'd be mad for a couple of days. Then life would go back to normal.

My mother was set up on a blind date with Joe Gimbel, an orthopedic surgeon. We would have a new normal. He brought us gum, drove a gigantic yellow Cadillac Eldorado, and was at our home for dinner every night. And slowly, very slowly, I started to accept the fact that maybe my biological father wasn't coming back, and that my mom had fallen in love with a man who was very happy to be our dad. Not too many other guys out there seemed to be looking to take on three extra kids. After three years of dating, my mom and Joe married and he is the man I call "dad" today. My mom sold our house, and the four of us moved into a home built into a hillside in the tony neighborhood of Paradise Valley, Arizona, with our new stepsister, Sari, and stepbrother, Mark.

The house sat on top of a hill, and you could see it from many points in the city of Phoenix. My dad had decorated the interior with a distinctly 1970s palette—lots of dramatic (and not in a good way) teals, cranberries, and greens. We had a live-in housekeeper, a huge swimming pool, a tennis court, and plenty of grassy areas where I would lie out and cook myself under the unrelenting Arizona sun, too absorbed in my teenaged ennui to notice I was burning. I shared a bedroom with Sari, whom I immediately dubbed "Fancy Sari" thanks to her incredible sense of style. A dedicated follower of fashion, she always had the coolest shoes, the cutest belts, and the trendiest accessories. When she stayed at her mom's, which was half the week most weeks, I missed her.

Every Friday night, the rule of the house was that you had to be at the table for Shabbat dinner, no matter what. It was a huge annoyance to me at the time, because I knew that all my friends were out having fun. My older brother, Mark, and I would fight over who got to say the prayer over the bread. If I was picked, I made sure to read the abridged version, as fast as I could, shaving precious seconds off the Friday night ordeal. My brother, on the other hand, would sing the whole prayer, and take as long as he possibly could, just to annoy me. The peak of my annoyance with Mark was reached when my parents decided he and I should share our bat and bar mitzvahs, because we were so close in age. I had imagined my bat mitzvah being the height of girlyness, all glitter and feathers and rainbows, the spotlight solely focused on me and my Gunne Sax dress. Instead it was an unglittery affair in colors of straight-up pink and blue, a marriage of total opposites—a little like my parents' approach to politics.

My dad was Republican, and my mom was a Democrat, so the dinner table conversation could get lively. A physician, my dad often talked about how public policy directly affected him, how it changed the way he billed clients, and how much he was taxed. My mom was much more concerned with social issues—she is pro-choice, and often said she could never vote for anyone who was anti-abortion. She voted with her heart, and my dad voted more with his head. I loved them both for remaining true to their personal beliefs. Despite being ideological opposites, they coexisted remarkably well.

As well as being a staunch Democrat, my mother harbored an intense fear of assimilation. If I brought home a non-Jewish friend, they'd have to be okay with being treated as though they were invisible. "Oh, who cares," is what my mother would say if I was crying over a boyfriend who was not Jewish. But if he was Jewish, it was, "Oh my God! How can we work this out?" Her grandmother had emigrated from Russia shortly before World War II, and she had been raised to never take her religion—and the ability for her to practice her religion—for granted. But as a teenager growing boobs and rocking braces in the 1980s, I had other things on my mind—like Guns N' Roses, and which high school football player was cutest. Besides, I knew better than to talk to my mom about her strict beliefs. My more diplomatic approach was to just do whatever the hell I wanted to, no matter what anyone said. Fuck the consequences.

Yes, I was fun-loving—too fun-loving some would say—which is why my struggle with depression didn't make sense to those around me. I had caring, supportive, and generous parents. A beautiful home. My teeth were getting straighter by the hour. How could I be depressed? I battled my dark feelings by being as impossible as I could be, turning my parents' beautiful teal and cranberry home into a latter-day Studio 54 whenever they were foolish enough to go out of town. After returning home to yet another scene of adolescent destruction, my parents decided enough was enough—their teenage daughter, who was drinking, cursing, and kissing far too many Gentiles for their liking, was to be sent away, to a special boarding school for kids with "problems." Shipped off to a *Girl, Interrupted*-type school in Louisiana at fifteen years old, I found myself in a uniquely enlightening environment, surrounded by a bunch of kids with more intense problems than I could have ever imagined having. Naturally, I gravitated toward the person my parents would disapprove of most—June Carson, a hard-drinking spawn of super-Christians with one year and eight lives' worth of experience ahead of me.

June was a pretty girl, with golden blond hair that trickled lightly over her shoulders and hung halfway down her back. Her bangs were a big mess of late eighties fabulousness, all teased and sprayed to perfection. Her eyes were swept with drugstore eye-shadow trios and her lips were always drowning in strawberry lip balm. At sixteen years old she smoked Marlboro 100's, swore, and was having sex with boys who wore earrings in whichever ear is not the gay one. She introduced me to AC/DC, MTV's Headbangers Ball, and hell—as in the opposite of heaven, giving me my first glimpse into Jesusland.

On a scale from 1 to 10, 10 being ultra-orthodox and 1 being the type of Jew who eats on Yom Kippur (fasting day of repentance), I clocked in at about a 5 (these days I'm more of a 6 or 7). I attended Hebrew school, had a working knowledge of the Ten Commandments, and understood that I was forbidden to eat bacon or shellfish, but wasn't exactly clear (at that time) why. I didn't, however, know shit about hell.

"You're going to hell," June warned, resting on her knees atop a white scalloped bedspread with lace edges. Since I didn't exactly understand the concept of hell—and my hymen, at this point, was still intact—I wasn't sure why I was going there.

"I don't think I believe in hell," I said.

"Well, you'd better start," she said, "because you're going."

June Carson came from a born-again Christian family. Her parents were missionaries who disappeared for weeks at a time to comb neighborhoods in foreign countries where they would spread the teachings of Jesus. That's why, I suspect, it was only natural, even for a rebellious teenager like June, for her to witness to a Hebrew on a humid Louisiana afternoon.

"Are you going to hell?" I asked, licking the remains of a Snickers bar off the tops of my pink polished fingers.

"Nope," she said confidently, "I've been saved."

Then she gave me a brief rundown. She sounded like an Avon Lady trying to sell an entire skin care and fragrance line. "First of all, it's very, very hot. You know how when you go to heaven you get a flowy gown and wings? In hell, you get the lower body of a goat, a pitchfork and a scrawny red pointy tail. There is no Mountain Dew, no boys, and no Def Leppard. It's round-the-clock misery mixed with fire and brimstone and you have to hang out with the souls of every evil person who ever lived."

Holy fuck. The lower body of a goat? That sounded a hell of a lot worse than the pear shape I currently contended with. No Sebastian Bach? No Def Leppard? How would I possibly ever be able to let another teenaged boy know how I felt about him if I didn't have Def Lepp's "Photograph" to dedicate to him during couples' skate? And the biggest bombshell of them all: There was no way I wanted to spend eternity with Jeffrey Dahmer, Ken Lay, and John Edwards. And P.S.: What the fuck is brimstone? June had made the sale.

Pushing all thoughts of my mother and Shabbat dinner aside, I got down on both knees at the foot of June's queen-sized bed and repeated her dictation, word for word: "At this time I would like to open my heart to let the Lord Jesus Christ into my life and accept him as my savior." I might be a Jew, and I might go to hell for being saved in an attempt not to go to hell, but I wasn't willing to take the chance. It was an approach to salvation that was similar to taking out an insurance policy on a home or car. You don't plan on your house burning down or a diamond earring being swallowed by a kitchen sink, but let's face it, shit happens, and in the event of unforeseen shit happening, it's good to know you're covered.

This paradox, the line between doing right and doing what was politically expedient, was a boundary I watched grow hazier and hazier as I grew older. Civic leaders, particularly the ones who weave salvation into their stump speech, did so, I believe, to give themselves the pass they need to act in their own best interests—not in the best interests of the public they swore to serve. For example, a Jewish Orthodox man (let's say, Jack Abramoff) may have bilked thousands of dollars from countless Indian tribes under false pretenses. That's okay, he rationalizes; he doesn't mix milk and meat. An evangelical preacher (Reverend Ted Haggard, for instance) may or may not have snorted crystal meth or had sex with a male prostitute, but on Sundays, from the pulpit of his mega-church, he warns against lust and sloth. Oh, and he never, ever, not even during the moment of orgasm, takes the Lord's name in vain (he's got boundaries). To them, houses of worship and the teachings that occur within them served as a sort of spiritual prophylactic to guard against retribution for their earthly deeds. Like a big latex moral condom.

While I was at the school, following in the footsteps of my good friend June the Baptist, I decided it was time I lost my virginity. His name was Tom, and he was the first boy who had ever paid attention to me. We listened to Guns N' Roses together ("our" song was "Sweet Child O' Mine"). He wore a jean jacket that smelled of rebellion, and I wore Guess miniskirts with bunchy socks, white Keds, a Liz Claiborne handbag, and corresponding strawberry-flavored and colored lip gloss. Tom had already had sex, and he made it clear that he would break up with me if I didn't deliver him my virginity, pronto. Of course, that was an asshole move, and if I had had any real self-esteem I would have told him to go fuck himself, instead of me. Instead, we "made love" in a van. I lost my virginity, gained a urinary tract infection, and he broke up with me anyway. Adding insult to injury, my parents had to be let in on the joke—I had to go to the doctor and get medicine for the UTI, and they were, subsequently, informed of my misbehavior. In those days you could get an abortion without telling your parents, but treating a UTI was a family affair. Considering I had been sent to reform school to get shaped up, not sexed up, my parents were, of course, disappointed in their wayward child. I was disappointed too. Not only had I been dumped, I'd been caught, a common theme in my life. I've always been good at getting in trouble—I've just never been very good at keeping it secret. Deception has never been my strongest point—ironic, considering my future career as a press tart.

CHAPTER 3

Pre Press Tart

My dad is a doctor. His dad was a doctor. My brother Mark, also a doctor, is helping in the fight to cure cancer. My baby brother, Scott, is an attorney; my sister Robyn, who has an MBA, is raising the next generation; and my other sister, Sari, is helping bring the arts to a community that had little. Clearly, I grew up surrounded by golden children who worked hard, made the grade, and toiled toward their noble goals. Me? I knew I liked hair metal bands, and that was about it.

Although I did halfheartedly attend college—I was always social, not scholastic, a polite way of saying I prioritized beer-chugging contests to attending class. The one thing I did hone at school was my talent for keeping up with current affairs. When my roommates creaked out of bed on Sunday mornings around 11:00 A.M. nursing themselves into recovery with a greasy breakfast and a Gatorade on the couch, I would already have been up for a couple of hours, watching *This Week* with Sam and Cokie, and *Meet the Press* with Tim Russert. I loved any broadcast (which was just about every) when Tim would surprise his politician guests with a quote on the screen from their deep and murky past. Words were weapons used to render the interviewees helpless; they became flies in the web of their own hypocrisy. I loved the game of it; the cutthroat, fast-paced, soap opera of American politics.

While my roommates swooned over Johnny Depp, I was having a torrid mental love affair with the *Wall Street Journal*'s John Harwood, a dreamy, distinguished man with a low, determined voice and impressive pedigree who was a frequent guest on my beloved *Meet the Press*. Tom Brokaw, Diane Sawyer, Christiane Amanpour, and Tim Russert—to me, they were so much more than broadcast personalities; they were portals, drawing me into living history. The threat of an arms race scared me much more than the sharpened fingernails of Freddy Krueger; in the nineties, my nightmares were about Operation Desert Storm and the Gaza Strip. I was young. I didn't have my own family. I didn't even have furniture. But for some reason, I was completely fascinated with the decision-making process involved in making policy. If there was one thing that my college experience taught me—other than how to subsist on Cheetos and Blue Gatorade—it was that politics, in the entire realm of human learning and endeavor, was the only thing in the world I actually gave a shit about.

The best thing about college, as far as I was concerned, was being part of a sorority, sharing that sense of sisterhood, camaraderie, and utter devotion to good times with girls who really seemed to appreciate me for who I was. Then as graduation loomed, something inside me clicked. I knew fancy-free was coming to an end, and that my share of the electric bill in the post-college apartment I shared with my sorority buddies wasn't going to pay itself. Time to find a career or at least a job.

In 1994, I left school, my dad gave me the push I needed to enter the real world, hooking me up with an internship in the office of Republican Governor Fife Symington's reelection campaign. He knew how much I loved politics, and arranged it through a guy who sat in the oak wood pew in front of us at synagogue. I had never seen a man with such extensive ear hair—it grew almost like Spanish moss, emanating from out of his eardrums, splaying on to the ear lobe and beyond. Who knew this study in human botany could be so well-connected? Well, he was. "Do you think you could use her help?" my dad whispered, loudly, in the middle of the Saturday morning silent prayer. "Sure," the man with the thick black ear hair said matter-of-factly, craning his neck to get a look at me. Monday I called, and Tuesday I reported for duty at the incumbent governor's reelection headquarters in downtown Phoenix.

Symington is a terribly nice man, tall with yellow hair and light eyes, who once rescued Bill Clinton from drowning, and would eventually become famous for his apparent interactions with UFOs. There was definitely something cosmic about him, in my twenty-two-year-old eyes at least—he was the first step on my stairway to political heaven. The "Fife Symington for Governor" headquarters were situated in an office space in a strip mall in downtown Phoenix—which is indeed as unsexy as it sounds. The magic happened in one big room, divided by a large partition, a Berlin Wall dividing the lowly volunteers and the senior campaign staff. When I arrived, I was on the wrong side of the wall—but not for long.

Every day, I came in around 9:00 A.M. and took my seat at the coffee-stained folding table alongside other volunteers—Gulf War veterans who lived off of their disability checks, senior citizens who had outlived their husbands, and bored housewives who had a few hours between carpools. Together, we stuffed envelopes and sealed them tight. We made copies, clipped newspapers, and answered the phone when the receptionist was peeing or having lunch. One of the veterans wore a baseball cap that read "Semper Fi," decorated with a symphony of military-themed pushpins documenting the wars he had survived. He warned me every day that if our Democrat opponent, Eddie Basha (owner of the Bashas' chain of grocery stores), won, I would lose my right to keep and bear arms. The moms complained that there weren't enough hours in the day to get everything done, and rolled their eyes when they talked about soccer practice and dance class. The senior citizens wore polyester pants and loose-fitting blouses with drawstring sleeves. They smelled like medicine and lotion, and often said how impressed they were that I was there, every day. I was impressed too. This was the first time in my life I had shown up for anything.

I looked forward to seeing my friends each day, especially the older ladies who made life in a retirement center seem peaceful and satisfying. My comrades in envelope-stuffing were at the conclusion of their lives and careers—but this was supposed to be a new beginning for me, and I had other goals—to bust through to the other side of the partition by any means necessary, to go from "aimless" to "top aide." After a few weeks of small talk with the volunteers, I hatched a plan to infiltrate; to break on through to the other side.

"No one will notice there is a twenty-two-year-old girl sitting in the midst of three press men," I reasoned. "And if they do, that's a good thing."

"Well, good morning, Lisa," the receptionist said. "Big mailing today?"

"Um, yeah," I said, walking through the double glass doors, forcing a wide smile. It was 7:30 A.M. and I was the first volunteer to arrive. "Walk casual," I told myself as I sauntered alongside the coffee-stained volunteer table, sliding my hand along the top of its rough surface. This time, instead of taking my usual place at the table, I kept walking. And walking. Right up to the dark faux wall that divided the room. A quick glance over my shoulder—and then I hopped into the Promised Land.

That was easy, I thought.

I saw three desks. One was hefty, dignified, and made of oak. It looked out of place in the squalor. The desk to its right was more in line with what you might expect from a temporary work space—small, beaten-up, and headed for the Dumpster once the election was over. The desk to the left was similar, except for the piles and piles of pink message slips scattered about, specters of calls left unreturned and meetings unattended. My Spidey sense told me this one had to be the desk of the campaign press secretary. With thirty minutes, until the good ol' boys arrived, I organized that desk as hard and as fast as humanly possible. When I had alphabetized the last of his to-do list, I heard the chirp of the alarm signaling the door had been opened to the campaign office.

"Good morning, Mr. Coughlin," the receptionist said.

"Good morning," I heard him say back.

I scanned the room for a chair. I found one, a folded one that was propped up against the wall. I quickly placed it next to a plant perch, which I had decided would be my desk. I threw the dying plant into the trash, placed my cup of coffee in the plant pot, and pretended to be looking for something in my purse.

Chuck Coughlin, the governor's campaign manager, was a stout man in his mid thirties with thinning hair. He wore a white, pressed, button-down, long-sleeved shirt, khakis, and cowboy boots. He didn't say a word, but I could tell by the way his eyes scrutinized me that my presence intrigued him—for at least two minutes or so. He sat down behind his desk (the oak one), fired up his computer, and worked away, as if I wasn't even there.

So far so good, I thought.

Twenty minutes later, the deputy campaign manager, Spencer, arrived. He was a little guy with chestnut hair and preppy round glasses. His pants barely touched the tops of his ankles. He was as sweet as he was awkward. He rounded the corner with a pile of crumpled-up messages in his hand and sat down. Five minutes later he swung his swivel chair around and silently waved at me while talking on the phone. I took my head out of my purse and waved back. The press secretary, Doug Cole, came in last. He was a tall, spindly man who also ignored me. They all did, for weeks. Then one day, Doug needed help.

"Spencer, can you come with me to the press conference today?" Doug asked.

Spencer looked awkwardly over at Chuck. Chuck looked right at Doug and pointed at me. "She'll help you."

My heart leapt.

"Yes. I will help you. Absolutely."

"Can you grab those?" said Doug, pointing to some equipment in the corner.

I lugged the heavy mult box (a piece of equipment used to deliver sound from the main mic) and microphone stand through a park in downtown Phoenix, sweat dribbling down my back, foundation melting in the broiling heat. It was one of the happiest moments of my life thus far. I saw huddles of men with tape recorders and television cameras gather in front of where the governor was to make his address. Following

Doug's example, I held up a blank piece of paper in front of the cameras to give the cameramen a white balance check. Grinning behind the blank piece of paper, I felt triumphant. Like I had found my place.

When the governor arrived, the pack of print, electronic, and television reporters fell silent. As he spoke, they rolled tape and took notes. At the end, they asked their questions and waited for answers. Sometimes they were satisfied, and sometimes they weren't. I watched the dance between politician and journalist unfold, and I felt proud, knowing that this moment was soon to be immortalized in print, and on television screens—and I'd help make that possible, even if it was mainly by shifting heavy equipment and holding a piece of copy paper. I felt possessed by the novice's fervor, that giddy sense that one may finally be a useful, adult member of society engaging in work that is "important." I wondered if this was the way my father must have felt the first time he performed surgery on a patient, or the first time my brother won a case in court. As I observed the ladies and gentlemen of the press, I enjoyed the gulf between "Us" (the governor and his minions) and "Them." I knew then that I had no interest in reporting the news; I wanted to make the news.

I started making friends within the campaign and among the local Republican party, and made an amazing discovery—there were others just like me! Namely, I wasn't the only political junkie who liked a drink or two—there were dozens of us out there! And possibly hundreds more, waiting to be befriended. Finally I had found a way to blend the two things I loved most—policy and partying. Election night was like college all over again—I spent it drinking beer out of a keg and smoking pot out of soda cans. I was part of a team, a unit, a group of people who had fought hard in the trenches to elect a governor. We were on top of the world—Fife Symington won, holding on to the governorship by a healthy margin, and rumor was he had the potential to be a future cabinet member for a Republican president. That was a good night.

"Lisa, have you thought about what you would like to be considered for in the new administration?" Chuck asked me, a few weeks after the election.

"No," I said.

"Not at all?" he asked again.

I knew it was called politics, the industry in which I was working. But now I understood what it really meant to be political and surround yourself with your own people.

"Well, I did think it might be fun to shadow the governor around for the day. I'd love to see what a day is like," I answered, thinking I had asked for too much.

"There is a job in the mail room, but I'll make you a part of the press office, too. At least this way you'll be on salary and you'll be down at the capital with us."

This was the first experience with reaping the rewards of my loyalty. Chuck could have easily given me a gift certificate to Ruth's Chris Steak House and a pat on the back, and I would've been thrilled. But he was loyal right back to me. My parents were thrilled—finally, their daughter was passionate about something that didn't come in a cocktail shaker. I had a whole host of new responsibilities: combing through national and local daily newspapers, compiling a clips packet for the senior staff, and occasionally Doug would let me write some talking points for the governor or tag along to an event. Most important, though—he needed his newspapers on his desk, every morning. So long as I did that, then I was the golden girl. And I nearly always managed to fulfill my daily obligation—the one time I didn't, it was thanks to Crazy Dave.

LIFE OF THE PARTY

I thought I loved Crazy Dave because he had a red Ferrari. David, or "Crazy Dave" as my governor's office staff renamed him, had come to Phoenix from Los Angeles to try and grow his money in the Phoenix hospitality industry. Crazy was tall with broad shoulders and sandy blond hair. "Who cares if he drives a red Ferrari?" I told my buddies at the governor's office prior to our first date. Well, apparently I cared a lot, because our first date went from zero to sixty in four hours. I had thought I was impervious to the seductive effects of a Ferrari, but I'm telling you: no woman can resist it, and I dare you to try.

I'd been dating Crazy Dave and his Ferrari for a couple of months when he called me at work with some fantastic news.

"I just bought a nightclub," he said. "I want you to see it, so I'll pick you up tonight after work and give you a tour."

I delivered the afternoon mail and made a beeline for the elevator before anyone could ask me to do anything else. I waved to the hidden cameras inside the elevators and pretended to flash my boobs. I knew that the governor's security detail monitored the elevators by closed-circuit television. Something else I can attest to: the best-looking men on any gubernatorial staff, red or blue state, is the security detail. They are the cream of the crop of state patrol cops, and they are hot as shit. They wear suits and carry guns. The answer is no, I never slept with one.

Back at my apartment, I stripped off my panty hose and threw my knee-length work dress across my bed. I grabbed a pair of tight-fitting jeans and a clingy white V-neck T-shirt. I always thought it would be fabulous to be the first lady of a bar. I could get all my drinks for free, and bouncers would have to be nice to me because I was dating the boss. I would have a wardrobe of fabulously sparkly barely-there outfits, and my own table would be tucked comfortably in the VIP section where I would lounge all night, accepting the well wishes of regulars, social climbers, and ass-kissers. If politics didn't work out . . . maybe Crazy Dave and I could start Phoenix's most glamorous speakeasy.

The Ferrari arrived and I was whisked away to the location. Turns out, he hadn't exactly bought a nightclub. He had bought an abandoned building that he hoped to, one day, turn into a nightclub.

"Here's where the bar will be," he said, pointing to a dark empty corner, and "over there will be the vodka lounge."

Cold vodka chased by frosty beers were sounding really good right about now, but since this dilapidated building clearly wasn't serving, I suggested we go find a functioning bar and celebrate Crazy Dave's future as club-owner extraordinaire.

After about the fifth lemon drop, I looked at my watch and noticed that it was midnight. I had to be at work by nine the next morning to deliver Doug's newspapers. While contemplating this reality, I had three more shots. Then Dave said it was time to go because instead of ordering my usual Grey Goose and grapefruit, I asked for "Another Grey Goose and vodka."

We cabbed it back to his apartment and were too drunk to do anything about anything, so we just fell asleep. I woke up the next morning at 8:40 A.M., which can also be read as *late*! Dave was still snoring when I realized that it was in fact a workday. It was looking very unlikely that I would be able to get up, get home, be showered, dressed, and at work by 9:00 A.M. All I have to do, I tell myself, is get the morning newspapers from the first floor to the ninth floor and on top of Doug Cole's desk. If they aren't there when he gets to the office around 10:00 A.M. he'll know I'm not at work and I'll be in big trouble. I don't want to get in trouble.

I hadn't had a drink in over five hours, but if given a Breathalyzer test, I would have probably blown a .14. This is the only way I can explain what happened next. I had no clothes at Crazy Dave's house, just what I was wearing the night before—a pair of jeans and a T-shirt that reeked of cigarettes and expensive perfume. Clearly, I couldn't wear jeans to the governor's office—how uncouth. So I went into Dave's closet, rummaged through his shirts, and pulled out what I thought would be an elegant alternative—a very long top that seemed like it could, in my pickled, hung-over state, pass for a dress. I had been known to rock the occasional micro miniskirt around the executive office, so I figured this wouldn't be too much of a stretch. I slipped the turtleneck over my head and looked in the mirror.

Yes, it is definitely quite short, I thought. *But it should get the job done.*

I slipped on my high-heeled loafers, and was out the door.

It was 8:55 A.M. I had safely scooped up the papers and was in the elevator on my way to deliver them. The doors opened and there I was, literally half-dressed in a black cotton mock turtleneck that I thought could pass as work attire, with major bed head and, from what I am told, record-breaking booze-soaked breath.

"Good morning," I said, trying to smile. My coworker Bettina took in the sight in front of her, got a whiff of the stink on my breath, and immediately fell to the floor in laughter. My other buddy, Trish, who took a more maternal approach to our friendship, was not amused.

"Gimbel, what the fuck are you doing?" she asked.

"I stayed out late last night with Crazy Dave. I think I'm still wasted and I have to get these papers to Doug's desk or he'll be mad at me."

"If Doug sees you walking around the ninth floor of the governor's office in your boyfriend's T-shirt and high heels, he won't be mad at you, he'll fire you."

With that, she took the papers and put me back in the elevator. "Get the fuck out of here. I can see your ass cheeks when you turn around," she commanded.

"Bettina thinks it's funny," I said, pointing at my friend.

"Well, it's not."

Still drunk, I giggled all the way back to my apartment to shower and change. Soon I was in agony, my head throbbing from too much alcohol. I grimaced through my headache when, later that day, Doug did ask me why Tricia delivered my papers, and was it true that I showed up to work earlier that day dressed inappropriately?

"Oh. I had just left my tights at home, and had to run home to get them."

Doug didn't seem overly concerned. He was too busy trying to run a governor's press office to be bothered with the case of the mail girl's missing hosiery. Halfway through his second term Symington would be forced to resign amid a savings and loan scandal—perhaps Doug had his hands full with the rumblings of that.

Crazy Dave never realized his dreams of bar ownership, and after three months, our relationship ended. I wasn't surprised. I should've known that if you get your bread buttered on the first date, your relationship is toast. But indirectly, Crazy Dave had helped me learn an important political lesson—if I could show up to the governor of Arizona's office in my boyfriend's turtleneck and not get fired, then I could land anywhere on my feet. There was only one logical next step: White House press office, here I come.

CHAPTER 4

Road Dirt and Fish Squirt

At twenty-four, I was the youngest person ever to work in the Arizona governor's campaign press office, and it was clear I was a Press-Tart-in-the-Making. I had an objective (White House press office), a slew of new friends who were just as geeky about policy as I was, and some real-world political experience under my belt.

Granted, the mail room wasn't exactly what you would call making it big, but it was more than I ever imagined possible. That said, when Doug and Chuck were originally selling me on the idea of coming to work in the governor's press office for $18,000 a year, I thought at the very least I'd have an office, a title, and the corresponding respect that comes with being twenty-two and a new taxpayer! Clearly there had been a miscommunication, because not only did I not have an office with a nameplate, I didn't have an office, period. My empire began and ended with a desk in the mail room.

When I wasn't sorting the day's deliveries, I was cutting out relevant articles for the gubernatorial staff (including the governor himself), and once in a while, Doug would throw me a bone and let me write a press release or some brief talking points. I proved myself to be a reliable foot soldier, which meant I was granted the honor of walking press releases over to the press corps office across the way, and I was always in charge of the mult box and microphone during press conferences. At least I wasn't fetching coffee, right?

After a year in Symington's administration, I resigned (if you can "resign" from the mail room) and packed my bags for DC, even though I didn't have a job lined up or any real idea of what I was going to do out there. But it was 1997, and I felt like time was ticking. Plus there was the small, ahem, legal matter in which Symington had become embroiled. He had been indicted on charges of extortion, making false financial statements, and bank fraud, and he was later convicted on the bank fraud charge. Symington had to resign. It was the first time I had seen the undoing of a man, close-up. (In January 2001 Symington was pardoned by President Bill Clinton, the man he once threw a life raft out to.)

When he announced his resignation, it came as a complete shock. Because I was not in the "inner circle," I only found out about it about an hour before he announced he was stepping down at a press conference. Like everyone else in his office, I was in disbelief. People were crying. *He is such a nice man*, I thought. *He was going to do such great things.* It was the first time I had seen the heavy political ax drop down on someone I knew. I hoped it was something I never had to see again, and packed my bags.

I kissed my parents good-bye, waved farewell to their pink palace, stuffed my earthly belongings in the trunk of the trusty Honda Accord my dad had bought me while I was in college, and put the car on a truck and had it shipped cross-country. I knew that I was leaving home for good—but for once in my life, I had faith that things were going to work out.

I arrived in DC a few days later, lacking any distinct plan but brimming over with excitement. My first few weeks were spent in an all-girl's hotel that Mom called the Barbizon. Those first few days in the nation's capital felt like first blushes of new love. I stood in awe at the foot of the Lincoln Memorial. I twirled through the decked halls of the National Gallery of Art, and stared, mesmerized, at the beauty and grace of Degas's *Dancers at the Bar*. Marching through the halls of the House of Representatives gave me goose bumps. I was humbled at the massive steps of the United States Supreme Court, and standing outside the iron gates of 1800 Pennsylvania Avenue, I whispered to myself, "One day."

But first things first. I found a data-entry job during the day and sniffed around for a way to join the political rat race. Volunteering, again, seemed the most direct route. It was at the time of the 1996 Republican primaries, so I signed up at the "Dole for President" headquarters in DC, working at night, figuring that I would be more likely to stand out that way. And if Dole made it to the presidential election, there'd be a good chance I could land a job on the presidential campaign. Which is exactly how it worked out—Dole was made the Republican party nominee in the presidential election, and thanks to the fact I had showed up to volunteer each night. I was hired as an assistant to Steve Goldberg, my salary bumped up to $25,000. At this point in my career, salary was less important to me than experience, which, I hoped, would lead to glory in the White House. For now, all I needed was enough money for shoes, dresses, and Pinot Noir.

Once again, I had springboarded from the volunteers' desk to the top floor of Campaign HQ, working for senior staff, trying not to choke on my coffee every time Newt Gingrich walked by, chatting to former secretaries of state. I'd bump into Elizabeth Dole in the bathroom putting her lipstick on, and we'd chitchat earnestly about her work with MADD, Mothers Against Drunk Driving. The Doles had a fat mini schnauzer named Leader who loved to come and hang out by my desk— probably because I kept a secret stash of treats on hand, just for him. I was surrounded by the cream of the Republican crop, and I loved it.

My boss, Steve Goldberg, was almost always in New York, so after a while he rented out my superior message-taking skills to Paul Manafort of prominent lobbying firm Black, Manafort and Stone. Paul was tasked with media buying for the Dole campaign, and I was given a desk just outside his office.

Rebecca Miller was an assistant like me, and our desks backed up to each other's. My desk was always lined with empty bottles of red wine, in homage to late nights spent at the office with Rebecca.

We were located on the top floor of the Dole for President campaign headquarters, right next to the CNN building. The CNN building had a fantastic salad bar, so fantastic in fact that Larry King's on-air guests could often be seen piling produce into a plastic container for a healthy take-out lunch.

Like the Reverend Jesse Jackson, for example. When we heard that Jesse was tossing a salad next door, Rebecca grabbed her Polaroid camera and we raced over to the salad bar for a photo op.

We made sure that our smiles were wide and our arms were firmly around Mr. Jackson. We wrote "HYMIE TOWN" on a piece of paper in black Sharpie and hung it, and our photos, above our desk. (Hymie Town—Hymie, meaning "Jew"—is what the Reverend had once dubbed New York.) We were so proud of ourselves.

"Girlfriend!" Rebecca called as she swiveled around in her chair to face me.

"What's happening, girlfriend?" I said.

"Look at this," Rebecca said, holding up faxed copies of the *National Enquirer*. I saw a grainy black-and-white picture of a bare-chested man and a woman with huge tits.

It was unclear what the trouser situation was for either of them:

"Roger Stone, as in Black, Manafort and Stone, has posted a naked picture of himself on the Internet and now he's in big trouble," she said.

Turns out Roger and his wife had placed a personal ad on the Internet in search of another couple—to swing with.

"Gross," I said, turning away like a vampire avoiding a crucifix.

"I know," said Rebecca, pretending to gag.

When the scandal broke, Roger Stone was let go from the campaign. But first they had to find him—to fire him—and make him go on *Good Morning America* to distance himself from Dole. He went missing—more like "into hiding"—for a little while. It was I who proudly received his first post-Internet-porn-site-scandal phone call into the campaign.

"Good morning, can I help you?" I said.

"This is Roger Stone."

"Who?" I said. "Roger? Roger Stone? One moment please." I put him on hold.

"Rebecca!" I yelled, hopping up and down and pointing to the receiver. She and I then spent the next three minutes running around the top floor of a presidential campaign, telling everyone that we had an Internet pervert on hold at my desk. Paul wanted to talk to him first, but Steve Goldberg was the one who had brought me here. "Dance with the one that brought you," they say. Once we calmed down, I patched the

Internet nudist through to Steve. It was one of the most exciting days of the campaign as far as I was concerned.

As far as Bob's chances in the presidential election went—well, everyone saw the writing on the wall. We may have believed that Dole would be a better leader, but it looked unlikely that he would be able to beat the younger, more dynamic Clinton. When Dole lost, I felt forlorn for everyone who had worked on the campaign, myself included. The lows, as much as the highs, injected my life with the kind of gravitas that had always been lacking in my safe, comfortable suburban upbringing. Dole's was the first presidential campaign I had been involved with—and losing hadn't in any way subdued my passion for the political game. On the contrary, the Russian roulette of it all thrilled me, and losing had only served to fuel my healthy masochistic streak. I wanted to do it again.

After Dole, I found myself fully aboard the campaign merry-go-round, alongside the legions of other young, smart, power-hungry kids like me. I found myself in pancake-flipping contests at smelly 4-H fairs; Saturday morning grassroots meetings at greasy spoons, where everything from the oatmeal to the toast is seasoned with pork; and the occasional state carnival butter-sculpting contest—some of the many stops on the typical campaign trail. I'm not trying to brag or anything, but I've seen a cow's udder made of margarine in a certain Midwest city (I'm talking to you, Iowa). This time felt like one long, carb-filled road trip through Middle America, filled with insight into how much simpler life could have been, had I not been so fucking focused. I met people who lived simple, un-complicated lives, lives that were about work and family and God. They never had to worry about carving an identity or a place in the world, be-cause they knew who they were from birth—they were going to be farm-ers, or raise livestock, and that was what their kids were going to do, too.

In 1997, I found my next gig—this time, in New Jersey working on the reelection campaign for Governor Christine Todd Whitman. A moderate Republican, she was New Jersey's first female governor, and under her leadership, pollution in the state had dropped significantly. I was thrilled to be working for a woman who had achieved so much. "What a coup!" I said as I packed myself, my clothes, and my hair dryer for a road trip to Lawrenceville, New Jersey, where I would be Whitman's deputy communications director for the duration of her reelection campaign. I would be taking a pay cut (Whitman was offering $22,000), but I figured the experience would be worth it in the long run.

The professional map I had planned out for myself was a series of moves designed to position me perfectly for a coveted spot on a presidential press team. I was always looking for a bigger and better media market in which to hang my hat. New Jersey was great—for two reasons, actually. The first is the Garden State's proximity to New York. New York is also known as media market number one. If you can work the New York press corps, you can work any press corps. The second reason is that 1997 was an off-year election. Off-year elections tend to be high-profile, if for no other reason than they are the only game in town. This particular off-year election featured a Republican woman: a rising star in the party, likely to garner lots of media attention. What was unfortunate was that Christine Whitman also happened to be a total fucking bitch.

Innocent of this, I drove my white Honda Accord to Lawrenceville, New Jersey, to meet my new boss: Communications Director Jacqueline Baim. She, like me, was a Dole alumnus. But all similarities stop there. Jacqueline was tall and gorgeous with an unruly mane of wild blond hair. She had a fantastic, ever-lasting set of legs that led perfectly into a butt no bigger than the palm of my hand. The quintessential New Yorker, she was tough and capable with a tender core that a select few were given the opportunity to see. While my experience was limited to being an assistant to someone important on the now-defunct presidential campaign, Jacqui was a bona fide superstar. She had been one of Bob Dole's traveling press secretaries. She flew aboard the campaign airplane, hobnobbed with the media elite, and rubbed elbows with the dignitaries.

Jacqueline was my boss and also my roommate. We rented a one-bedroom apartment in Lawrenceville that was built uncomfortably close to a humming set of power lines. Jacqueline paid $75 more rent a month than I, securing herself the master (and only) bedroom. My sleeping quarters was portioned off of the living room with a lattice wall. My room had everything I would need during my stay in New Jersey: my thrift-store mattress, my hair dryer, a chair, and a full-length mirror propped up against the wall for hair drying. In high school, my exhaustive hair-drying efforts earned me the "Best Hair" award—the teenaged equivalent of the Nobel Peace Prize.

Jacqueline and I were at our desks in the Whitman for Governor headquarters from 7:00 A.M. sometimes up until 9:00 P.M. By the time we got home from work, we were starving and neither one of us was interested in cooking. That's why, once a week we would overorder Chinese takeout and keep the leftovers in the fridge for quick and fast dining. At any one time we would have three quarts of Szechuan chicken, two quarts of hot and sour soup, way too much beef and broccoli, and lots and lots of white rice in the fridge.

What we lacked in vitamins we did not make up for in décor. Our apartment remained bare until the lobby of the apartment complex underwent a complete aesthetic makeover. The apartment landlord—whom we called "the lovelord" due to the thing he had for Jacqueline—gave us the discarded lobby furniture: two wicker armchairs and a burgundy floral love seat. We were living high now! For a while, we had a third roommate after I brought home a fish from a New Jersey state fair (campaign appearance). I named it Seacacus (after a county in New Jersey). Seacacus lived for three days and died of accidental overfeeding.

Jacqueline was the Batman to my Robin. It was my first real press job, and she showed me the ropes, and helped me out when I got stuck. And boy, was I proud of myself when I managed to score some good press for our candidate. I even adopted a wall in the campaign office that I dubbed the "Gimbel Wall of Fame," covered with stories from newspapers in which I was quoted or photographed. One photo was of me, strapped to a stretcher—Whitman was at an event where a first-aid demonstration was held, and guess who volunteered to be the CPR guinea pig?

As much as I adored Jacqueline, it was hard working for someone (Whitman) who treated her campaign staff like dirty laundry, with her nose pinched and her head held high up in the sky—not exactly the picture of tolerance and compassion I had been expecting. Whitman seemed to think it was beneath her to talk to us, even if we were sitting in a car with her. She would behave as though we weren't there, even avoiding eye contact. On the one hand, I understood that maybe she wasn't interested in taking direction from a twenty-four-year-old girl like myself. But to treat Jacqueline, a well-known and respected professional, like an insignificant Smurf seemed plain rude. She exuded a smugness that implied she was so confident of her reelection (even though she only won by half a point, in the end) that she didn't see much point in suffering a campaign staff.

There was one person who loved Christine Whitman, however—Howard Stern. It was I who bore the responsibility of booking her on his show. He was so very respectful and supportive, it was almost disarming.

Whitman won the election, and as soon as the votes were in I started looking for another job. I found one in Vista, California, working in the office of Viper car alarm magnate Darrell Issa. This race marked Issa's first run for elected office. He sought the Republican nomination for United States Senate to run against the incumbent Democrat, Barbara Boxer. Three moves in, I had this packing-my-life-up-on-a-moment's-notice thing down to a science.

After finding out I got the job (my salary would be pushing a handsome $28,000), I called a trucking company so I could have my car shipped out to where I was going. Normally I would bring a mattress and rent furniture, and probably find someone on the campaign to be my roomie. But in California, things were a little easier—my parents had a condo on the beach in Coronado! So what if it was a forty-five-minute commute from the tiny island off of San Diego? I was twenty-six years old living in a condo on the beach by myself! I didn't have to pay rent or utilities, and my entire paycheck went toward putting gas in my car and buying clothes, and now bathing suits. I couldn't have been happier. My commutes were spent drinking coffee and losing myself listening to San Diego's alternative rock station 91X; my workdays were, well, spent working; but my weekends were spent by myself, in my bikini, on the beach. I wish they all could be California jobs!

And this time, my job was more high profile than it had been thus far—I was Issa's press secretary, my words were on the record, and I was the official go-between between the media and the campaign. A millionaire, and a very nice man I might add, Darrell Issa poured $10 million of his personal fortune into the primary campaign—but it was money maybe not spent so incredibly wisely.

Darrell had made his money as the inventor of the Viper car alarm system (he is now a Congressman), and it was his voice that countless wannabe car burglars heard telling them to "please step away from the car." Despite his wealth, Issa lived in a modest home and had a sweet, down-to-earth wife. The one thing he didn't have at the time was experience.

New on the scene, he hadn't yet fully defined who he was as a politician and as a conservative. Someone gave him the advice that he should focus on his "nice guy" credentials. He was ahead in the polls when Issa went ahead and green-lit some unfortunate commercials, one of which was a sort of "blooper reel," showing outtakes from his previous campaign commercials, proving what a likeable guy he really was. It creeped out conservative Republicans, pundits, and voters alike, who were scratching their heads, wondering, *Why is this guy doing a blooper reel, when he's running in a large state, in an important election, trying to defeat Barbara Boxer?* Then it came to light that in 1972, he had been convicted in Michigan of possessing an unregistered handgun, and put on three months' probation. This didn't help his chances.

Issa lost the primary election by five points. Had we won the Republican primary, my career would've been helped significantly. But we didn't. So, I packed my bags, updated my résumé and looked for the next job. I hopped aboard U.S. Congressman Jim Lightfoot's campaign to become governor of Iowa, and found myself in Des Moines. Ah, Des Moines. It's exactly how you would imagine it. Endless fields of corn and soybeans. While waiting for my car to be trucked in, Lightfoot's wife kindly lent me their 1974 blue Buick, which sometimes started and sometimes didn't. I was sharing an apartment with a fund-raiser and the candidate's assistant—he slept on the couch. As always, my furniture was limited to a mattress and a full-length mirror. That's all you need— oh, and a hair dryer, of course. The campaign fell short, as it wasn't clear if we were really "for" anything, and we had a strategy as devoid of charm as those soy fields.

Lisa Baron

In the space of two years I worked for four different campaigns, traveling the country, waking up early to go to state fairs, hand out propaganda, and field questions from journalists all day long until at some ungodly hour, I'd unfurl in a bar with my cohorts and a Grey Goose cocktail, pondering what the next day might hold. What makes most Americans uncomfortable—unpredictability, job instability, and chaos—made me thrive. The hustle and bustle of campaign life, coupled with constant radio and television coverage, made me feel alive, not anxious. What I feared more than unemployment was unfulfillment. Life on a political campaign was akin to what I imagined life on the road with a rock 'n' roll star is like if you are a part of the backup band: screaming crowds, groupies, paparazzi, motorcades, police escorts, private airplanes, alcohol, VIP treatment everywhere you go, drugs, adrenaline, hangovers, fast food, sex, and inappropriate conversation (sexual harassment is as commonplace around a campaign office as staplers and copy machines). Luckily, inappropriate conversation has always been a special talent of mine, and I could always give as good as I got. The only real downside to being on the road, as far as I was concerned, was having to use public restrooms—one of a few phobias of mine, along with air travel, heights, and not having a hair dryer.

This love of the game and the push to make it to Pennsylvania Avenue led me to accept a job as communications director for the Republican Party of Florida (Jeb Bush was the newly elected governor). Finally, the big break I had been looking for: a livable salary—$40,000, which could bring me to my second life goal: my first Prada bag. Plus, I could afford an apartment that I could call my own. It was a shame my new job happened to be in the armpit of the free world. You're probably thinking, *Bitch, quit your crying and go have a Mojito in South Beach.* I would agree with you, except that the job I accepted was not in Miami or anywhere near it. I would live and work in Tallahassee, Florida. Yes, Talla—fucking—hassee, where every day is a carbon copy of the day before: hot and muggy with a fifteen-minute thunderstorm around 4:00 P.M.

As soon as I arrived in town, I had a feeling I wasn't going to fit in. I was at the bank, opening up an account, when the teller started having a conversation with someone who clearly was not there. I wasn't quite sure what to do, so I just waited until she was done chin-wagging with her imaginary friend.

"I'm sorry," she said turning back to me.

"Um, that's okay," I said, forcing a smile.

"Are you Christian?" she asked me.

I'll admit—I had not been expecting to get into any kind of theological conversation that afternoon.

"Baptist?" she asked.

"No," I answered, really wishing I could just deposit my check and leave.

"Protestant?"

I am not exactly sure how many denominations of Christianity there are, and I wasn't interested in sticking around to find out.

"I'm Jewish," I said. She thought about it for a moment.

"You know, I was just talking with Jesus and he was telling me that you are a really nice person and I should talk to you about his teachings."

"Sure." I said resignedly, as she wrote her phone number down.

Welcome to the South, I thought.

As much as I tried to fit in, I was miserable in Tallahassee, verging on clinically depressed. And I did as much self-medicating as legally allowed. Even the weekends provided little respite from my boredom. I usually spent them by myself, daydreaming and eating whatever the grocery store had priced to move in the takeout section. Usually it was chicken wings, lasagna, or three-day-old egg rolls. Regardless of the menu, I always bought three bottles of Pinot Noir and ice cream.

Once home in my third-story apartment, I would slip into some pajamas, apply a cucumber face mask that I picked out of the dollar sale cart, and settle in for a weekend of loneliness. On the rare occasions I did go out, I almost always ended up wishing I had politely declined.

"Come on, Lisa, just squirt!"

One lamentable afternoon, I found myself at a barbecue with a garden hose in one hand and a squirt gun in the other, being forced to squirt a goldfish through the hose until it popped out the other end. Whoever's fish made it through first, was the winner. I could hardly believe that this was what was considered entertainment among the people I was associating with. As we stood there with our hoses, drinking to get drunk, I wondered who was having a worse time—me, or the fish—and decided it was a tie.

It was around this time when Ralph Reed's office called. And I answered.

CHAPTER 5

The Right Hand
to God Knows What

"**D**avid with the Republican National Committee is on line two!"
buzzed the Florida Republican Party receptionist, Darque-
sha. Hot-ass David Israelite (who surprisingly enough, with a
name like that, is not a Jew) was on the phone. My heart pounded. David
was the guy whom I was kissing until shortly before my first liaison with
Ari. He was the political director for the Republican National Committee, and was what I dreamed my husband would be like: tall, handsome,
smart, and funny. I got so excited about the thought of David becoming
my betrothed that I stuck my three-inch stilettos right into his sides like
a couple of spikes on the back of a pair of bull rider's boots, so as never to
let go. It turns out, men don't take kindly to this particular type of aggressive entrapment. Regardless of the fact that I spent far more time
stalking him than actually dating him, he cared about me enough to do
something about my low quality situation in Florida. He knew how much

I hated my life (and job) in Tallahassee, and it was he who gave me the heads-up about an opening with Ralph Reed's lobbying firm, Century Strategies, in Atlanta, Georgia. David Israelite, the non-Jew, I have you to thank for my induction into the world of right-wing Christian Fundamentalism.

"This is Lisa," I said, casually, as though I had no idea who was on the line.

"What are you wearing?" he asked in his cool, low, sexy voice.

"Hi, David," I cooed.

After a few minutes of idle chitchat, he laid it on me: "Ralph Reed is looking for a communications director."

I had no response.

"Do you know who that is?" he questioned.

"Yes, of course I know who he is, the devil, that's who," I said.

"Well, if it's alright with you, I'd like to forward the devil your résumé."

"Look, David, you and I both know I'm a complete mess. I drink like a fish, I'm not exactly a virgin, and I can't speak in tongues—not to mention that I don't even really know what that means."

David couldn't argue with some of my main points.

"Yes, Lisa, you have some behavioral issues, but you are a very smart girl and you are good at what you do. Besides, everybody knows that Ralph is in George W.'s inner circle and that the campaign listens to what he says."

"But he's the Right Hand of God," I whispered. "Don't you think it would be weird?"

Me, work for the man who had picketed abortion clinics, and probably has the book of Genesis on CD for long road trips? And then there was my pro-choice, Democrat mother—what on earth would she think?

David thought I was worrying too much.

"Lisa, this is politics. Who cares? I mean, aren't you already in hell?"

Yes, Tallahassee—my own living hell.

David told me the deal: Reed's office wanted someone with a drive that only a twentysomething could muster, and who would prevent any shit-storms from tarnishing the company halo. They were also looking for a candidate who could facilitate media and public relations projects for Ralph's high-profile corporate clients. Plus he'd be paying close to $50,000, more than what I was making while festering in Florida.

I thought about it. Over the last year or so, my career had felt like a series of bad decisions, from Whitman (I often say she's like the UN, only bracketed by a *C* and a *T*) to life in Florida (so close to sea level, creatures on the evolutionary ladder don't have to climb very high to get there). Hmm. Maybe going to work for Jesus Christ's chief henchman was a divine means to my happy ending. I wanted someone I could believe in for real this time, someone who could stay true to a core set of values (without expecting me to, of course): honesty, compassion for the young, weak and old, someone who possessed a true calling to improving civic life. A person who could stay focused on legislation, and not the long legs of a twenty-five-year-old House staffer. Yes, Ralph was one of the more polarizing political figures in recent history—"I do guerrilla warfare," he said of his approach to politics, back in the heady Coalition days. "I paint my face and travel at night. You don't know it's over until you're in a body bag." But guerilla or not, as far as I could tell, he was a devoted husband and attentive father. Plus he was close to the Bush clan, and George W. was already on his way to winning the Republican nomination in the 2000 presidential election. It might not be such a bad idea for me to jump aboard the next phase of Reed's stellar career.

I'll work for him for a year, I thought. *I'll do a really good job and then call in my favor. "I would love to go to the White House," I'd tell him. And he'll say, "Yes, Lisa, you have been so loyal, I'll get you a job in the Bush administration."*

As promised, David sent my résumé over. Ralph called, and shortly afterward, I was on my way to Georgia for my interview with the man himself. It was scheduled to take place in the Atlanta airport, in the Delta airlines conference room, and I flew up from Tallahassee just for the afternoon. It wouldn't be the first time I had seen Reed in the flesh—that had been a few years earlier, in San Diego for the Republican National Convention. I saw him getting out of a car and blustered, "Shit—that's Ralph Reed! How can something so handsome be so evil?"

A few years later, when I was already working in Florida, I spent an evening with Reed and some friends in a bar. It was during another Republican conference and Ralph, who had quit his hard-drinking ways and found God years earlier, was the first to leave. I, on the other hand, closed down the bar with MSNBC's Chris Matthews. At 6 A.M. the next morning, Ralph and I were on the same shuttle bus headed for the airport. He looked at me and laughed. "You looked a lot better last night." And here we were again, sitting face-to-face in an airport lounge in Atlanta. I hoped he had forgotten me and my hangover from the shuttle bus.

"Let's go through your work history," he said, looking at my résumé. "Dole, Whitman, Issa—wow, that's quite a losing streak you're on." He started laughing.

I was horrified. Yes, I'd had a history of attaching myself to losers, thus far. Plus, Whitman was a moderate, pro-choice, unlike him. He gave me a writing assignment—an op-ed piece that he asked me to write when I got home. I went back to the Tallahassee heat with my assignment, certain I wouldn't be getting the job no matter how good my writing was. Three days later, the phone rang. It was Ralph.

"Welcome aboard," he said. I hadn't realized it would be that easy to sell my soul.

When I went to work with Ralph, I traded in my political roadie status for a desk job, a salary, health insurance, and free sodas in the fridge. No more blue jeans and tank tops in a temporary office that was being rented by the campaign from a big donor. It was skirts, Spanx, and stilettos at Reed's Century Strategies, a grassroots firm that sold advice to Fortune 500 companies and carried out direct-mail operations for political campaigns. I would still be swimming with the political sharks, but this time from a cage that could be pulled out of the water and into safety with the tug of a rope. And if I had to swallow it all down with a couple of "Hail Marys" and an "Our Father Who Art in Heaven" every now and again, that was okay with me.

CHAPTER 6

Are You There, Godaphile?
It's Me, Lisa

Ready to start afresh, which I hoped and prayed would be devoid of all forms of goldfish torture, I packed up my white Honda Accord again, and left Tallahassee with hardly a backward glance. My car had seen better days—the tinting, which we had gotten in Arizona, was peeling off, and my tags were expired. But I stopped worrying about getting pulled over the second the freeway fed me into Atlanta and I laid eyes on its glittering downtown skyline. I immediately felt at home in this new city—even if my new boss was the most divisive Bible-thumper in the history of New American Christianity.

Ralph Reed—truth is, as much as he is considered a hero by some, there are plenty more who would love to see him water boarded. On the strength of dogma, Ralph brought political polarization to the mainstream in the 1990s, and he did it with style. Smooth and dapper, an Evangelical Rudy Ray Moore of sorts, he wears alligator skin boots on his feet and Christ on his sleeve. With his baby blue eyes and impeccably styled hair, he was the perfect poster child for the large faction of conservatism that had, until he came along, been known for being angry, intolerant, and disheveled. He captured the country's attention at the tender age of twenty-nine when he was put in charge of televangelist/would-be president Pat Robertson's Christian Coalition, which held the sway of a social conservative mega-voting block able to decide who would be sent to Capitol Hill and who would be sent home packing. Vehemently against abortion, gay marriage, stem cell research, and all forms of social liberalism, the Christian Coalition was the political mouthpiece of middle America. As its leader, Reed made Republicans (the social conservatives, at least) swoon, Democrats puke, and broadcast journalists drool all over themselves, hoping to grab a few words with him either on or off the record. He was the ultimate Godaphile: one that has a near-obsessive affinity for—you guessed it—Him.

These are the people who stick "God" bumper stickers on their vans, sing along to Christian rock, fasten "Jesus First" lapel pins to their suits, and watch *America's Got Talent*. I found them intriguing—they are firebrands, obsessed with promoting Jesus and his agenda from the moment they wake up, while urgently making peace with their own paths in life. For many Godaphiles, it's not enough to simply be a regular person. They have been singled out by the Lord, and as such, their lives have special meaning and purpose that transcends the ordinary. And they're usually more than happy to tell you all about it.

While I do enjoy me some food for my soul every now and again, clearly I am not a Godaphile. I am a press tart, a twentysomething secretary/spokesperson who, if asked, would be hard-pressed to explain how they qualified for their jobs, let alone who God really is. Even so, Godaphiles and press tarts enjoy a symbiotic relationship. Godaphiles appreciate us, not just because of our heavenly short skirts and fitted shirts that grip a pair of divine young tits—but because they need us. After all, you can't hire a Godaphile to do the devil's work. And Godaphiles are far less inclined to end up getting bent over that big wood desk after hours.

For the politically minded Godaphile, a good press tart is one of the most vital parts of their toolbox. As media corporations have grown increasingly underfunded over the years, their thirst for scandal has intensified. Scandal sells. Elected officials seem to be constantly hounded by journalists, so they are always hounding their press secretaries to defend their honor, often at all hours of the day and night. Throw alcohol and hormones into the mix and *bam*! You've got yourself an unholy union of flesh and tongues. While Godaphiles and press tarts commingle to help form the nation's laws, it's not true that the political process is reserved solely for the stately and the slutty. Take forty-eight-year-old former pageant queens like Ralph's personal secretary, Big Les, a perfect harmony of height, beauty, and crazy. If she were a wine, the sommelier might describe her as a full-bodied blend of decrepitude and dependability, with lingering notes of compassion and menopause. Recently divorced after twenty years of marriage, she was always trying to lose weight and subject to hot flashes and mishaps that resulted in a constant stream of unintentional comedy that she brought to work with her every day, along with her lunch.

"Can you believe I work for Ralph Reed?" she would roar with bewilderment as she hung up the phone with Former House Majority Leader Tom DeLay's office.

Big Les had been with Ralph since Century Strategies opened its doors in 1998. She wasn't religious. At Century Strategies, you didn't have to share Reed's views; you only had to share his work ethic. Which worked out just fine—we were a bunch of heathens and we didn't care about divine retribution, so long as we got everything done by 5 P.M. Thanks to Big Les, e-mails would occasionally be forwarded to the wrong set of eyes, faxes would be lost in transmission, and business flights intended for Boston were ticketed to Birmingham. But that didn't matter—she was loyal. And loyalty, in Ralph's eyes, was the most valuable trait an employee could have. It wasn't something that could be taught (unlike faxing or not hitting "reply all" on personal e-mails). And Reed, in return, was loyal back. He helped Big Les out financially, and vowed that wherever he went, she always had a job. The last part wasn't necessarily an act of chivalry—his last two receptionists, after answering phones for three months, had gotten knocked up. Since Big Les was in her late forties and hadn't had sex (with a partner) since her divorce, the risk was low that she would put in for maternity leave. She might, however, put in for a mental health day, since her patience was constantly being tried when it came to the rest of the Century Strategies team, or "you girls" as she called us.

"Where you goin'?" Big Les yelled from her office, which sat directly across the hall from mine and next door to Ralph's. "You girls got another two-hour lunch?"

"Um, no, I am actually taking my very first client trip to DC," I said, closing the door of my corner office, with its faux gold-framed pictures of flowery pastures. The décor smacked of mass manufacturing and low-rent Laura Ashley, yet it was a welcome departure from the chaotic interior design of a campaign office, which had more in common with a teenage boy's bedroom. There, you might find decaying pizza stapled to the wall. Or a dead fly in a jar, meant to symbolize our intentions for the opposing campaign. Anyhow, there was no need to call on my inner interior decorator, as I wasn't planning on staying in Atlanta too long.

I could hear Big Les's voice trailing me down the hall like the train of a puffy-white wedding gown. "You girls don't do any work with your lunches and your trips . . ."

There are a few thousand things I'd rather do than fly, like give a stranger a foot massage for one. I realize commercial air travel is not exactly a new concept, and yeah, I understand that statistically it is safer than car travel blah blah blah. But for me, I've never gotten over the feeling that I'm in a small tube en route from the car window to the bank teller. So, to take my mind off being trapped in a cylinder at 35,000 feet, I play a game with myself called, "Which Flight Attendant Is Banging the Captain?"

"What can I bring you?" the petite blonde in the fitted airline uniform and coordinating cotton apron asked after I'd settled in my first-class seat.

"Bloody Mary mix, please, no ice." I sized her up as she walked away, wondering if she was the one. Unless it was the chirpy redhead with the boob job who greeted passengers at boarding.

Before becoming a press tart, I used to travel in coach. I'd always wondered who sat in first class, and why. Why would anyone pay for a weekday-upgraded ticket to Reagan National Airport when everyone knows the cheap way is coach into Dulles? But now the hot towel was in the other hand. I smiled at each main cabin passenger who trudged past me, wondering if they were thinking about who I was and why I was sitting in first class on my way to the nation's capital. Was I a lobbyist? Was I the head of communications for one of the many Fortune 500 companies headquartered in Atlanta? Was I an heiress to an oil fortune? Or was I just another traveler who had cashed in her SkyMiles for a free upgrade? No, I was Ralph Reed's right-hand woman, and I loved that as well as traveling first class, Chris Matthews's and Larry King's producers were calling me, wanting to set up interviews with Ralph. Thanks to my boss, the cream of the crop of political journalists, the people whom I once watched all day while on my couch at college, were phoning me.

Corporate life, I was finding, had other great perks, like expense accounts, and workdays that abruptly ended at 5 P.M. no matter what was on fire. And to my relief, the environment at the office wasn't as ultra-religious as I had imagined. In fact, Ralph was exceptionally respectful of my faith, however casually I practiced it. An interesting thing I learned about evangelicals is that they love Jewish people. They are pro-Israel, because they believe that God promised it to us, and they also think that Jews are the chosen people. Which was handy when it came to vacation time—Ralph said I could take every Jewish holiday off, and if I had to leave early for Friday night dinner, he was fine with that, too. Before taking the job with him, I had half-wondered if he might try to convert me. But nothing like that ever happened.

With my peppery tomato juice in hand, I rested my head on the crinkly airline seat back sanitation paper. The redhead, I decided, was banging the captain, for no reason other than she was a redhead, and men like redheads, especially ones with fake boobs and giggles. I opened my computer bag and pulled out the itinerary Big Les had prepared for me. It seemed I had a luncheon with some Catholics at 1 A.M.

Ah, Les, I thought. *I really do love you.*

I tucked the schedule into the seat pocket in front of me, accepted a refill from the redheaded home-wrecker, and stared out the window, waiting for our nation's capital to emerge from beneath the clouds. We landed at noon, and by 12:30 P.M. I was in a Lincoln Town Car on my way to an advertiser-appreciation luncheon for *Crisis*, the nation's leading Catholic magazine. I filled my mind with virginal thoughts, and rationalized my behavior in advance. *Well, at least they're worshipping a Jew.*

CHAPTER 7

Holy Shit

Everything I learned about other religions, I picked up on the playground or from June Carson. Pentecostals handle snakes. Southern Baptists all live in Louisiana or Mississippi with at least one Ku Klux Klan member per family tree. Allegedly, Christians don't drink. But Catholics drink a lot. (Remember the old joke, wherever you find four Catholics, you'll find a fifth?) I hoped the Catholic stereotype was true; that the pope's people like to booze it up. Maybe I'd be sandwiched between a Grey Goose vodka exec and the director of viral marketing for Budweiser at the *Crisis* magazine luncheon. We'd drink our way through the afternoon, hit up some happy hours, then party on through the night until the wee hours. But no, at 1:00 P.M. I took my seat between the public relations officer for the United States Conference of Catholic Bishops and the assistant to the director of the Washington, DC, Right to Life Organization. Which is not what you'd call a party. I buttoned up my shirt, for the love of God, and banished all thoughts of happy hour from my mind.

"Let us bow our heads in thanks," the priest in the black jeans said.

The only noise in the room during the pre-meal prayer was the clanking of dishes being handled by the waiters and waitresses who hung in the shadows outside the swinging kitchen door. I tilted my head, not comfortable with engaging in the full-on bow. I didn't want my Jewish God to think I was bowing before an idol. I hoped he'd realize I was simply participating in social grace, not actual grace. Besides, pretending to pray came with the job.

I took the opportunity to scan my black wool pencil skirt for traces of lint or puddles of spilled coffee. My eyes slowly moved from my calves, then my knees, to my thighs and over my rounded hips to the intersection where the top of my skirt met the bottom of my white satin camisole. I came to the conclusion that if you didn't know me, you might think I was a real estate agent who used her sex appeal to sell homes.

"Lord, we thank you for this food that is about to nourish our bodies," he continued.

I slipped on the pin-tucked tailored jacket I had draped over my chair, transforming myself from business-slutty to evangelical ready-to-wear in a blink of an eye.

"We are grateful for this sustenance we are about to receive, and we ask that you keep us strong, focused, and principled as we work, here in this glorious nation's capital, to serve you."

My glance surreptitiously danced around the plain conference room, looking for another set of twitchy eyes. *Is there someone at this lunch who shares my fear of assimilating during Christian prayer?* Negative. I looked back down, checking my cell phone for missed calls.

"In your name, we give thanks to our Lord, Jesus Christ, and let us say, amen."

"Amen," said the woman to my left with the regal puffy white hair and sensible shoes.

I smiled at her.

"Are you with the magazine?" she asked, her shiny gold cross bobbing at her neck.

"No," I said, closing the complimentary copy of *Crisis* that was placed on my chair.

"An advertiser?" she continued.

"I'm here representing my boss, Ralph Reed. He and the editor are very close friends."

"Oh," she said with dawning respect. "We really need him working as hard as he can to elect Governor Bush," she continued.

My boss was one of the strategists to the presumptive Republican nominee for president of the United States, George W. Bush. In no uncertain terms, he told the country that Bush would provide the holy Southwestern elixir we needed to shake that nagging eight-year hangover from all the immorality of the liberal Clinton administration. But before he could become the forty-third president of the United States, he had to win the Republican primary. Every Republican primary candidate, from Family Research Council President Gary Bauer; my lipstick buddy, the Red Cross Executive Director Elizabeth Dole; had wooed Ralph Reed. If you scored Ralph's support, you were automatically privy to the gallons of blood, sweat, tears, and votes of Ralph's army of social-conservative followers. In the end it was Bush who won the affections of the Christian king. (Reed later told me he had chosen to work with Bush over the other candidates because God had spoken to him, and explicitly instructed him to do whatever it took to get George W. Bush elected.)

"We are working very hard. I believe with all my heart that George W. will be our next president," I said.

"Finally, someone we can be proud of in the White House," she said, her cross clanking against her chest as she grew animated.

"Would you like sweet or unsweet tea, ma'am?" the white-coated waiter interrupted.

"Just some more coffee, please," I replied.

I checked my cell phone to make sure I would not be late for my next stop: overseeing production for a segment of Channel One's *Best Friends* show. Channel One is a news network tailor-made for kiddies, and was another one of Reed's clients.

I made my way over to pay Ralph's regards to the editor of *Crisis*, Deal Hudson, a heavy-weight authority on all things Catholic. "I'm Lisa, with Ralph Reed's office," I said, extending my hand. "I'm so sorry he couldn't be here today."

"Nice to meet you, Lisa," Hudson responded, his eyes waltzing up and down my torso. He was very nondescript, like a rental car.

"I'm glad you could be here. Did you get a copy of the magazine to take back with you to Atlanta?"

"I did," I said, my scarlet-red fingernails pointing to my brown Furla briefcase.

"Please give Ralph my best when you see him," he said with a wide grin.

"I will, and thank you so much for having me here today. It was a lovely luncheon." Then I made my way outside and hailed a taxi.

I couldn't wait to get out of there. As the cab sped and braked through the District, I rolled down the window to let the cool air run across my face. I hadn't experienced anything quite so pious in my entire life. And I'd never faked anything quite so hard . . . not even an orgasm . . . not in the name of God, anyway. I knew I'd better get used to it. I slipped on my oversized tortoiseshell Ralph Lauren sunglasses and reminded myself that at least I had no drama, no scandals, no psycho candidate's wife undermining the campaign strategy, and no prep-school interns to baby-sit. And not only that, I was working for Ralph Reed, someone proven, someone with integrity, someone I could believe in even if I didn't believe that God has a son named Jesus.

I pinkie-promised myself that I would perform the most stellar, professional, and impeccably perfect job that I was humanly capable of carrying out for Ralph and his big-paying clients. It was important that I impress him; that way once George W. Bush was elected president, Ralph would call in a favor to his buddy to make sure the White House Office of Communications hired me. I tried not to lose sight of that and my ultimate goal: White House Press Secretary. I visualized myself standing behind the dais with the Presidential Seal in the White House briefing room. I mentally riffled through scenes and the wardrobe I would need in order to speak before the citizens of the United States of America. Outfits would be planned around the news of the day. Anything war-related called for a well-tailored suit; a black silk, long-sleeved blouse; and a St. John's catalog pair of leather platform heels. An economic crisis called for a Diane von Furstenberg patterned cotton-spandex blend dress that wrapped my five foot, seven inch frame in a serious yet "no need to get crazy" manner. Weather or other natural disasters, most notably wildfires, required something more sedate: a sensible navy pant-suit and crisp, white button-down shirt with French cuffs and black patent flats. Earthquakes called for a knee-skimming skirt, a jewel-toned sweater, and a pair of Gucci high heels. Each outfit would resonate with the pièce de résistance: a long strand of pearls, à la Barbara Bush. I imagined myself calm and poised. I would point to anxious journalists, taking each one of their questions on topics ranging from North Korea, global warming, and eradicating evil, to the Dow Jones and offshore oil drilling. I'd trot out answers as if I was ticking off a grocery list. This fantasy was made extra-delicious when I envisioned myself providing Republican women an alternative to the angry, long-haired, wild-eyed Ann Coulters of the world—she always looks as though she's just been dropped off from the night before. When it came to Republican women, there was a loss of perspective. Sturdy and austere women dotted the halls of freedom and occupied the stools of the local bars and happy hour haunts. This explains the pandemonium a swatch of blond hair can cause. Our party needed women who were devoted to lower taxes and Brazilian waxes! We needed on-camera spokeswomen who wanted to paint the country and their lips red!

Lost in my reverie, I hadn't noticed that we'd arrived at the location of today's Channel One shoot: a public elementary school. I paid the driver and looked for the administration office, so I could get my visitor's badge and meet the rest of the crew.

"Hi, Lisa for Channel One," I said to the woman behind the desk.

Channel One delivered news to elementary-school children in digestible kid-friendly segments. You may have heard of some of the people who cut their journalism teeth at Channel One: Serena Altschul (MTV), Maria Menounos (*Access Hollywood* and *The Today Show*), Anderson Cooper (CNN), and a young Lisa Ling (*The View*, National Geographic Channel, and *Oprah*). Primedia, Channel One's parent company, is a $70 million media company headquartered in New York, and they retained Century Strategies to consult on more family-friendly content, and tackle any uprisings from social conservatives, should they occur. Senator Richard Shelby from Alabama, for example, thought the channel was promoting violence and encouraging underage kids to watch inappropriate movies. So Primedia had asked us to come up with some good, clean, pro-family content to counter the negativity. I was there to ensure Ralph's vision was being applied.

Only I had to keep quiet about who I worked for because of the reaction the name *Ralph Reed* sometimes brought out in people, especially those who saw him as a zealot, a religious boogeyman shoving his morals and virtues down America's secular throats. People usually fall into two categories: they think Ralph Reed is a Christian using politics to push a Godaphile agenda, or they think Ralph Reed is a politician using Christianity as a Machiavellian tool. Over time, I learned the type of person who would be impressed when I told them I worked for Ralph Reed, and the type of person who would be horrified. Or which person would call the *New York Times* to tip them off to the religious political leaders' work on behalf of a big liberal company. And what would the "Old Grey Lady" do with this information? Publish it with the same frenzy Bob Woodward ran with Watergate. Guaranteed. As such, I was not, as requested by my client-contact Primedia, to publicly mention that I worked for Ralph under any circumstances. They were scared to be associated with Ralph because he was a firebrand, but behind closed doors, they were happy to pay him to keep the wrath of socially conservative America at bay.

"Am I the first one here?" I asked.

"No, there is a man with a camera," she responded as she led me into a quiet library. Sure enough, there was a man with a camera.

"Sharon will be here soon, she's with the talent," he said, setting up his lighting.

Sharon was a beautiful African American woman with a big purple scarf around her neck and a soft voice. Her hair was blown out straight and came to a complete stop at her shoulders. The talents were two anchors, a man and a woman.

"They're married, but they don't want anyone to know," Sharon instructed. "It's bad for the image they have. Well, you know, they want to seem young enough to be credible to kids."

Believe me, I understand living a double life. I was going to spend the next hour or so pretending to be familiar with abstinence, for goodness' sake. The show would feature tweenage girls talking about how to just say no. Lucky for the girls, I was not going to be involved in the interviewing. Had I been, I might have told them about how the "69" position is a lie. ("Your boyfriend will tell you that you will both have fun. He's wrong. It's impossible to enjoy anything when you have a hairy, low-hanging ball sack in your face.")

Five girls aged around twelve came bounding in through the doors. They took off their jackets and mittens and placed them neatly on a nearby table. They began gabbing, gossiping, playing with each other's hair, and checking out who had the better-smelling lip gloss. They were innocent and sweet and all thoughts of me wanting to tell them not to pretend they like blowjobs to get a boyfriend flew completely out the door.

The girls spoke clearly and confidently into the camera about the power of friendship and the self-esteem needed to be strong against outside pressures—namely boys and drugs. As I watched the interview wrap up, I hoped they would remain innocent for as long as possible. Although I do think there is merit in testing out the goods before you get hitched—I mean, who wants to spend all eternity married to a tiny penis?

On my way to check into my hotel (the Willard Hotel, thank you very much), I checked in by phone with Ralph to let him know that everything went great today.

"The luncheon was very nice, and I made sure to check in with Deal Hudson for you," I said.

"He's a great friend," Ralph responded.

"The Best Friends segment shoot was wonderful. Those little girls are very special. I'm going to type up a memo for the client to give a run-down of the day, but wanted to let you know first."

"Thanks, Lisa, good work," Ralph said.

"I'm back in the office tomorrow," I said.

"Right," said Ralph.

I hung up the phone and began to devise a plan to get my hands on a big fat glass of Pinot Noir. The word on the street is that the plush, patterned fleur-de-lis carpeting of the Willard Hotel has felt the footsteps of DC's most influential feet. I'd heard your chances of bumping into a United States Senator, presidential cabinet member, or network news correspondent roaming the plush-carpeted halls of the Willard were always high. I raced to my room to transform, Wonder Woman–style, from Holly Golightly into Holly Goloosley.

I was getting dressed and in the middle of a beautiful daydream about how I would buy a new Tumi carry-on suitcase and bill it to one of Century Strategies' clients when I heard the Samba ringtone on my cell phone go off. "RR Cell" appeared in the caller ID.

Motherfucker.

I must have done something wrong,

Very wrong.

OMG.

I am getting fired.

Deal Hudson probably told Ralph that my areolas could, in fact, be seen through my shirt and some nuns were complaining.

Or maybe the conversation I was having in my head about that dastardly 69 position was really out loud. Please, God, say I didn't say "sphincter muscle" in front of those tweens.

I white-knuckled my cell phone as I put it up to my ear.

"This is Lisa," I said.

"Yeah, Lisa this is Ralph Reed. I need you to return a call to Joel Brinkley over at the *New York Times*," he directed from Atlanta.

"Oh," I said collapsing with relief into an overstuffed chair.

He continued, "It seems someone has tipped him off that we are doing some grassroots consulting for Microsoft. See what Joel wants and call me right back. This isn't good."

CHAPTER 8

Out of the Closet

In 1998, the United States Department of Justice and twenty states filed an anti-trust lawsuit against the Microsoft Corporation. The software giant was being accused of running a monopoly by linking their Windows operating systems with their Internet Explorer browser on Intel computers. This practice, the government alleged, restricted the market to competing browsers. Microsoft, in part of an overall defensive strategy, hired my boss, Ralph Reed, the Right Hand of God, to orchestrate a grassroots lobbying campaign. The aim was to get high-profile people of faith to write letters to congressmen and other important lawmakers who might be sympathetic to Microsoft or, in their positions as legislators, could have a say at some point in the court battle or future legislation. Still with me?

The case, and Ralph's lobbying, coincided with the upcoming presidential election. While George W. Bush had not yet been anointed the

Republican nominee for president of the United States, he was clearly the front-runner. And Ralph was a top consultant to the presumptive nominee. This is why the *New York Times* was calling. You can imagine the chubby a reporter would get just thinking about catching Bill Gates, Ralph Reed, and George W. Bush in bed together. Can you say "wet dream"?

Newspapers and magazines were, at the time, swirling around the drain of a collapsing industry. Nationwide, they were losing subscribers by the thousands. Copy editors, advertising staff, and those in administrative positions were disappearing off of the company payroll. Reporters, always the more tenacious type, knew what was needed to keep their jobs: blood. Nationally the *Los Angeles Times* and the *New York Times*, once beacons of truth and objectivity, were outing CIA operatives and exposing intricate terrorist finance schemes without regard for the consequences. Desperate to remain relevant, these one-time journalism behemoths were acting out like promiscuous sorority girls. She might say (rather, slur) that the walk of shame is fun, but all signs indicate a cry for help.

What made matters worse was that when we received the call from the *New York Times*, it was 4:00 P.M. Most newspapers require that all stories be submitted by around 5:30 P.M.-ish so that the copy editors can tidy up the text, and the next day's newspaper can begin to take shape. A reporter (particularly an investigative reporter) calling so close to the filing deadline could only have meant one thing: this douchebag had already written the story and was calling more as a CYA ("cover your ass," if you don't know) operation than as a fact-finding mission. Even so, I wasn't about to just lie down and let the *New York Times* try and destroy my boss's credibility.

I dialed the 212 number Ralph gave me.

"This is Joel," the voice on the other end answered.

"Hi, Joel, this is Lisa Gimbel with Ralph Reed's office. I understand that you are working on a story."

"Um, yes. Is Ralph available to talk?" he asked.

"I'm so sorry," I said, actually sounding like I was sorry, "but he's not. He asked me to give you a call."

"Okay, well then, I got a tip that Ralph has been hired by Microsoft. Can you confirm this?"

"Let's do this," I said. "Let me have all of your questions, and I will go and get you all the correct answers you need. I want to make sure I get you the absolute facts." (That statement, by the way, is code among press secretaries and reporters for: *I am a peon who is not authorized to say anything until I have consulted with someone higher up the food chain.*)

Joel rattled a litany of questions including, "How much does Microsoft pay Ralph a month?" and "Does Governor Bush know that Ralph is being paid to lobby him directly?" The line of questioning suggested that this reporter wasn't just seduced by the thought of catching these three men together; he was already lying in bed and smoking a cigarette.

I called Ralph, recounted the conversation and the questions, and listened to what he had to say. Calmly, he gave me instructions, none of which I questioned. His confidence soothed me. He was right, they couldn't touch us. After all, he was Ralph Reed, Jesus' homeboy, a proven conservative leader whose political career had been the subject of an entire edition of *Time* magazine.

I called Joel back.

"Hey, Joel, this is Lisa with Ralph's office. I have the answers to your questions."

"One minute while I pull up the story," he said. "Okay, I'm ready."

"Unfortunately, Century Strategies has a policy of not discussing the work we do on behalf of our clients. But I can tell you, off the record, that Ralph was absolutely not hired for the sole purpose of directly lobbying George W. Bush on behalf of Microsoft."

"So, you really haven't told me anything," he said.

"Look, Joel, off the record, I know you want this kill, but the facts just aren't there. You probably think that I just say and do whatever I can, even if it's not the truth, because Ralph signs my paycheck. But in order to 'lobby' you have to be a 'lobbyist,' and to be a lobbyist on behalf of any company, especially one as giant and under the microscope as Microsoft, you would need to register as a lobbyist. Ralph is not registered because Ralph is not a lobbyist. He conducts grassroots lobbying campaigns, but he doesn't personally lobby. If you print that he was hired to personally lobby Bush you will have printed something inaccurate. Again: Microsoft did not hire Ralph to whisper sweet anti-monopoly nothings into George W. Bush's ear."

Silence on the end of the line. And then, "Okay." It sounded like he was processing what I had said, and might even be considering the information.

"How do you spell your name?" he asked. My heart stopped. My name? Me, in the *New York Times*? My elation was overshadowed by the terrifying vision of my mother opening the newspaper and seeing my name alongside Ralph Reed's. But what could I do? Deny Ralph in his moment of need? I hadn't heard any cocks crow, but still—I refused to go the way of Saint Peter.

"Lisa Gimbel. G-I-M-B-E-L."

I called Ralph back to tell him about the conversation.

"I don't think I talked him off of the front page of this non-story," I told him. "I'm really sorry."

"It's the *New York Times*," he said, "and you did your best. All we can do now is wait and see what kind of fires we will have to put out tomorrow."

And then he dropped the real bomb on me.

"Now, I need you to call Ari Fleischer over at the Bush campaign," he said. "We need to make sure we are on the same page with the campaign before we release our response."

I couldn't believe my boss was making me call the guy I had given head to. In those days, sex didn't mean anything to me. I worked very hard to make sure I didn't get my feelings hurt, which was easily achieved by not having any feelings in the first place. I avoided intimacy like the plague, and if I actually liked somebody (which was rare, but happened; see David Israelite) the best I could do was try to be a little less dismissive than usual. But there are unforeseen consequences to being a stone-hearted press tart, no matter how watertight your emotional armor may be. One of them is being forced to call the guy you're supposed to be ignoring. I made the call, and left a message with his assistant, specifying that it was Lisa Gimbel from Ralph Reed's office, calling on a matter of urgent business. Not Lisa Gimbel, from the hotel room in Greenville, calling to arrange another late-night hook-up. Oh the shame. Shame that was compounded when, days later, Ari still had not returned my call. I was horrified, relieved, and then horrified again. It was looking more and more likely that Bush was going to be president—by blowing Ari, had I blown my chances of a White House press gig?

(Note to self: If you are going to sleep around, sleep around with Democrats. There are many reasons for this, such as: I've never seen a

Democrat wear a bow tie, Democrat men tend to wear their hair longer and shaggier, and the risk factor of having to be the one to call first after performing meaningless fellatio in a South Carolina hotel room is statistically insignificant—or so I'm told. But then, math has never been my strong suit.)

CHAPTER 9

Forgive Me, Mother,
For I Have Sinned

I was one morning newspaper away from having something in common with Clay Aiken: being forced out of the closet by the media. My parents knew I was working at a political consulting firm called Century Strategies in Atlanta, but I hadn't gone so far as to tell them that the president of Century Strategies was Ralph Reed, a general in Jesus' army.

My mom, Marilyn, is a petite blonde who has weighed the same (extra-small) since forever. This small but mighty ball of maternal instincts can make everything feel better or the world feel miserable with one look. My dad, Joe, is an orthopedic-surgeon-turned-businessman with a predisposition for gently herding and shuffling his five kids along life's playing field, stopping only briefly for lectures on why his life choices should be ours, and the importance of sticking to a sound monetary budget. I believe he was a border collie in a previous life.

LIFE OF THE PARTY

My parents are both second-generation Jews whose respective grand-parents (both sets of whom died before I was born) escaped Eastern Europe at the beginning of World War II, when Jews could still get out alive. The American Dream, to them, didn't have as much to do with chicken in pots and two cars in a garage as it did about being able to openly practice their religion without threat to their lives or livelihood. In my undereducated opinion, Americans tend to be passive with a right, but more protective with a privilege. And to my parents, their Judaism is a privilege, one that they trusted their Semitic spawn would protect, particularly in today's mixed-up world where anti-Semitism is seeing a comeback, assimilation is commonplace, and intermarriage is a virus. Yes, my folks really fretted about their offspring wandering too far away from the Torah, or Arizona. I probably made them fret the most out of all my brothers and sisters.

I started realizing I was different right around the time I got boobs, and it wasn't because I went from ant bites to a D cup in a summer. There was always something inside me that itched to fly the nest. What makes most Americans feel nervous makes me feel alive. And in campaign politics, the restless little bird inside me had found the perfect place to land. The fact that no two days were ever the same suited me. Fueled by coffee, Diet Coke, cigarettes, and adrenaline, there was always a fresh fire to extinguish, new public policy to introduce, or some incredible news to leak to the media. The thrill of the ride, the late-night strategy sessions, the constant public relations crises made me feel alive. By choosing to work for a Christian icon, I wasn't being rebellious; I was being me. Besides, Ralph did have his good points. He was smart, determined, focused, and successful. And with Jesus as his copilot, I was confident that he practiced safe business. All this in mind, I picked up the phone and punched in my folks' 602 number. I had to confess before the *New York Times* piece came out the next day.

You may be wondering how it could be that I hadn't shared with my parents who my boss was. The answer is, they never asked. Every time I took a job in a new city, my parents only ever had one concern: "How many Jews live there?" They would be happy—or not so happy—depending on the number of synagogues per square mile. When I moved to DC, it was, "Oh my gosh, there are 200,000 Jews living there, wonderful!" New Jersey—"Fahget aboudit!" Everyone is a Jew in New Jersey. When I moved to California, due to the inflated Hebrew population near the beach, they encouraged me to spend more in San Diego and less in Vista. Whenever I moved, my mom's primary concern was that I join a synagogue and find a husband as soon as possible. Tallahassee they were not excited about in the least, so when I told them I had gotten a job in Atlanta, they were thrilled. "Atlanta has at least a hundred thousand Jews," my mother exclaimed. They were so pleased. The more Jews, the more chances I might have to join a synagogue and find a husband.

I started the call off the way I always did: I said hello, and then immediately tried to deflect attention away from myself and onto a sibling.

"Hi, Dad." I was thankful that he had answered, and not my mother.

"Hey, Li, what's going on?"

"Nothing much, how about you?"

"Your mother and I were just going through some old boxes, getting ready to move out of the house while the renovations are going on. What are you up to?"

"Not much," I said.

"Have you met anyone?" he asked.

"No . . ." I said, wondering how far my eyes could roll back in my head. As I neared thirty, "Lisa the Wayward" was rapidly evolving into

"Lisa the Spinster," in my parents' ever-worried eyes. I was sick and tired of being the black sheep, to tell you the truth.

Robyn, my eldest sister, is the quintessential firstborn: semi-parental and nauseatingly responsible. Sari, sister number two, was rebellious but better dressed than I, and scored points by marrying a blue-eyed South African Jew. My brother Mark is my parents' dream child: a surgical oncologist with a wife and three kids. He once, while attending college at the University of Michigan, grew his hair long—and that was about as far as his ventures into subversiveness went. Scott, my younger brother, is the baby of the family. Three days before any familial birthday or anniversary, he usually texts me to see what I've done in recognition of the impending occasion. "I already signed your name to the card, loser," I text back. "Send me fifty bucks to cover your half of the gift." Somehow the check always gets lost in the mail, and at last calculation he owes me approximately $217,056.34. Then there is me. I wear my skirts too short, my heels too high, I drink a little too much, kiss a bit too often and, not to mention, too soon. It was Scott I hoped could, this time, save my ass.

"So, what's Scott up to?"

"Oh, he's great," said my dad.

"Oh." There was nothing for it—I'd have to confess and get it over with. "Well. I was just calling to check in, see how everyone is doing, tell you a little bit about work."

"Have you met someone in the office?"

"No. Well, I've met some people, but I have not met the person you are referring to." I continued, "Um, did I ever tell you and Mom who the CEO of Century Strategies is?"

"No, I don't think so," said my dad.

"That is so weird!" I said with perplex in my voice for believability. "I could've sworn I said something. Well, I totally doubt if you have ever heard of him, it's really not that big of a deal, he's not an elected official or anything, he is just this guy named Ralph Reed," I said, my voice trailing off.

"Ralph Reed? I know who that is!" exclaimed my dad. "Oh, Jesus, Li," he said with a laugh, "your mother is going to have a fit."

The next thing I heard was the plunk of the fiberglass phone hitting the Corian followed by hurried footsteps across a hardwood floor.

"You have something to tell me?" The unmistakable boom of my mother's voice.

"Um, I'm pregnant?"

The phone line went silent. My mother had always wanted grandkids, and once told me that if I became pregnant out of wedlock, we could always pretend that the father had been lost at war. I could hear the wheels of her mind turning, thinking about which wars were currently under way.

"No, not really, Mom. I am working for Ralph Reed, though."

"Christian Coalition Ralph Reed? Oh my God!"

"Yes, that's the one," I said. I think she would have been much happier with an unwanted baby.

"*Lisa!* First you tell us you work for Republicans . . . and now this?"

Judging by the pain in her voice, an eavesdropper might have assumed I just told my mother that I had been arrested for soliciting sex with minors on the Internet, clubbing baby seals, or denying the Holocaust.

"I wanted to tell you guys now, because tomorrow I am pretty sure I am going to be quoted in the *New York Times* as Ralph's spokesperson. I thought you should hear it from me rather than read it in the newspaper."

"I can't say I'm thrilled" she said, passing the phone back to my father without saying good-bye. My mother has always had the ability to make me feel about the size of a very small, undeveloped pea.

My dad came back on the phone.

"Terrible, just terrible," he lamented, waiting until my mother was out of earshot.

"Wow, the *New York Times*!" he whispered. "That's great, Li! Go get 'em."

I held back a few tears and laughed.

"Thanks. I'll try."

Chapter 10

I Suck

Apparently, I suck at giving head. Why else wouldn't Ari return my call? Believe me, I would rather get tea-bagged by Kamala the Ugandan Warrior than be the first one to call any guy post-hook-up. But even if he had returned my call, I doubt it would've helped Ralph. The story, as we anticipated, ran on the front page, above the fold. The headline screamed: "Microsoft Hires Bush Adviser Ralph Reed to Lobby Bush."

Fuck. I sat on my living room floor in my pajamas, clutching my morning coffee in one hand and the newspaper in the other. I scanned the rest of the six-hundred-word story, trying to assess the damage and figure out how to handle the damage control, when I came across my contribution.

"Today, Mr. Reed declined to talk about his company's contract with

Microsoft, saying (through a spokesperson) 'We have a policy of not discussing our clients.'"

Spokesperson? WTF? What happened to "How do you spell your name?" Asshole. The least they could've done was give me my fifteen minutes, especially after I'd already gone and preemptively outed myself to my parents. I felt like such an idiot.

My cell phone rang. It was Ralph. Calling me at 8 A.M. Sounding grouchy.

I have learned over the years that the inflection in Ralph's voice when he calls me is usually a good indicator of the type of day I am about to have with him. His greeting never began with a "Hello" or "How are you?" It was always: "Hey."

A low monotone "Hey" preceded by silence means that today is going to be bad.

An easy, but pointed "Hey," means that everything was fine.

A quick, gruff "Hey" means annoyance. Somebody somewhere had fucked up somehow. And today, I feared it might've been me.

I answered the call.

"This is Lisa," I said like a soldier reporting to duty.

Silence and then a baritone "Hey." It was gruff. Most definitely gruff. Gruffer than a billy goat with blue balls.

"They really screwed us," Ralph said.

"I am so sorry," I said, my voice heavy with failure. "I really tried to talk him away from reporting false news."

"I have a breakfast this morning, but I should be in the office around nine o'clock. When you get to Century, come into my office and we will see what we can do about this," he said.

We hung up the phone and I kicked my morning ritual into high gear.

I didn't know what could be done to repair the damage that was already shooting around the Internet at lightning speed. I did know that I hoped this mess could somehow be fixed. How could Ralph recommend me to the White House Press Office if I couldn't even handle this? Maybe this was an opportunity for me to show of what mettle I was really made.

Since I knew I would for sure be seeing Ralph today, and would be performing vital career damage control on behalf of both of us, I made sure to dress for the occasion. A climate-controlled bra was essential; you wouldn't be able to tell by looking at my nipples how hot, cold, or terrified I was. I threaded each arm through a fitted baby blue cotton blouse and shoved each thigh into a pair of extra-small Spanx. Nobody likes a panty line, not even GOD. I tucked my ironed shirt into a pair of black Theory pants I found lying on top of a stack of clothes back from the dry cleaner. (Or was it my "needs to go to the dry cleaner" pile? I didn't have time to worry about it right now.) I looped a black and white thin snakeskin belt through the waist of the pants, slipped on a pair of three-inch heels, grabbed my keys and my cigarettes, and headed out the door. With my triple, no-foam, one Equal latte, I arrived at Century Strategies, ready to put out some hellfires.

I rode the elevator up to the ninth floor and swung open Century Strategies' oversized wooden doors with the appropriate amount of drama. It took three hard right turns to arrive at Ralph's office—and it could take anywhere from five to forty-five minutes to get there depending on who you bumped into on the way.

"Lisa Gimbel, what on earth are you doing here?" Big Les shrieked from the conference room.

"Yes, I'm early. Gotta take care of some business with Ralph."

The Century Strategies conference room was the first thing a person saw when they entered the office. It overlooked the parking lot and parts of Duluth, which lived up to its name by being truly one of the dullest suburbs in the city. It held a large meeting table that could seat six, a set of matching armoires, and a television with cable. This is why Les was in there, so she could watch television while she ate breakfast.

"Ralph Reed called me real early and said he was going to be in, too," she said. She always referred to him by both his first and last names. "I guess you guys have a busy day ahead!"

I looked down into her bowl and saw what I imagined three bears might eat for breakfast. It was yellow, mushy, and turgid. It looked like popped zits.

"What on earth is that?" I said, swigging my Starbucks.

"You never seen grits before?" she asked, as though I had just asked what year it was.

"Les, I'm from Arizona," I said.

"Well, honey, I'm a Southern woman and Southern women must have their grits. They won't affect my diet because if you are going to eat carbs, you're supposed to eat them before noon."

I didn't know where to take the conversation from there so I just brought it back to the entire reason why we were all at work before 9 A.M.: Ralph.

"So, is Ralph here?" I asked.

"Yes, Ralph Reed is in his office," she said, sprinkling more salt onto her Southern breakfast.

I turned right and headed down the narrow hallway toward Ralph's palatial office: the epicenter of this multimillion-dollar political consulting firm.

The large corner office gave its occupant a view of every quadrant of Atlanta. An exquisite hand-carved mahogany desk with soft edges and perfectly chiseled details commanded most of the room. Stacks of paper were organized on top of the desk, and phone messages were neatly piled in descending order down the right. Four newspapers waited to be read on any given day. Behind the mother lode of a desk was a coordinating credenza that gave support to matching sterling-silver Tiffany frames. The largest of the frames elegantly offered a large black-and-white photo of Ralph's fair-skinned, ginger-haired bride, JoAnne, whom he married when she was nineteen and he twenty-six.

I set my venti latte down on a glass coffee table and gazed at the rows and rows of photographs on his French Vanilla office walls. Ralph with President Reagan; another one with Mrs. Reagan; one with President Ford, President George H. W. Bush, Former Secretary of State Condoleezza Rice, Newt Gingrich, Pat Buchanan, and ultra right-wingers Phyllis Schlafly, Dr. James Dobson, and convicted Watergate-conspirator-turned-prison-minister Chuck Colson. It was a mini-Smithsonian of the Godaphile class.

Ralph was pacing behind his desk, talking into a mouthpiece that wrapped around his head like adolescent head gear, discussing the *New York Times* article with a prominent Bush financial donor, assuring him that there was no truth to the story. He waved at me and I took a seat on the leather couch, watching his every move. This was a different side to Ralph. I knew he cared about power more than money, and that was one of the things I liked about him. But he needed money—from companies like Microsoft—to get the power. Perhaps more than I had realized.

Ralph removed his headset and moved around the corner of his desk. His tan Brooks Brothers slacks were meticulously pressed and held up by a worn leather belt with a gold buckle. A green Ted Baker oxford hung lazily off his upper body. The honeyed hue of his skin gave away the weekend's golf game that was probably played on the Arnold Palmer golf course that backed up to his gated community home. He replaced his headset with a wireless BlackBerry earpiece, but instead of taking a seat in the wingback chair that never saw an invited guest's ass (that was Ralph's chair), he breezed past me and shut the door. I froze. This usually meant that I was about to be fired, forgiven, or molested.

"What do you think we should do, Lisa?" he asked, crossing his two-inch-heeled crocodile boots, a large bottle of Fiji water in his hand.

I breathed a sigh of relief. He wanted to hear my opinion.

"Well, I know we said we had proof that we weren't hired to directly lobby George W. Bush, but, um, do we?" I asked with uncertainty in my voice.

"I think I can get something that'll work," he said. "I hope the governor (referring to George W. Bush) and Karl (referring to Karl Rove) aren't upset." And then he asked rhetorically, "Do you think they are upset with me?"

I shook my head no, but really I had no fucking idea. I didn't know Governor Bush or Karl Rove, and I didn't find out until a few years later that it was Karl who had gotten the Microsoft business for Ralph in the first place. At the age of thirty-nine—following on from being on the cover of *Time* magazine at thirty-three and heading the Christian Coalition at twenty-nine—Reed had allied himself with one of the most powerful political families in America.

"Call Joel and tell him that we need the name and telephone number of his editor," Ralph instructed. "Then we'll kill him."

When it comes down to it, I'm not afraid to cut a bitch, but no actual bitches were cut in the aftermath of the *New York Times* scorcher. Here's how it actually went down, with me following Ralph's instructions to the letter: I called Joel and got his editor's name. We sent them a copy of a letter written by a prominent social conservative also stating that the story was factually inaccurate. Our point was, the focus of the Century

Strategies campaign was not, as the story had stated, to bend Bush's ear. That would mean Reed was lobbying, which he wasn't, technically. What he was doing was indirectly lobbying. The gray area that his work fell into was his defense, and it was wrong, we insisted, for the *New York Times* to print that the "aim of the campaign was to curry favor with Governor George W. Bush." The editor reviewed the facts as we presented them, and the next day this item ran in the paper:

The New York Times, Wednesday, April 12, 2000

CORRECTIONS

A front-page article yesterday about a lobbying campaign by Microsoft misstated the company's explanation at one point for hiring Century Strategies, Ralph Reed's firm. As the article noted, a Microsoft spokesman said Century Strategies' specific aim was to counter a lobbying campaign against the company being waged by its competitors. The spokesman did not say that its aim was to curry favor with Gov. George W. Bush.

More people are likely to read the entire dictionary than the corrections page of a major metropolitan newspaper. In fact, many readers have no idea there even is a correction page. It's usually the last section of any major newspaper and printed in very tiny letters. But we didn't care—we had gotten our correction. Ralph was happy again, happier than I'd seen him in a while. His very own press tart had taken on the behemoths at the *New York Times*, and won. She had big enough balls to call up a big-shot reporter and defend the honor of her boss. I was delighted to be on Ralph's good side again, and imagined Joel cowering in a corner as his editor loomed over him with a whip, ready to administer fifty lashes. Which I guarantee did not happen. He probably got promoted.

Ralph spent the day forwarding the correction to his conservative colleagues and friends. He even sent me an e-mail, titled "thank you." He acknowledged my hard work and said that had it not been for my tenaciousness, the situation, now contained, would've been much worse. I received the e-mail at 12:51 A.M. on Thursday, April 13, 2000, and I still have it to this day.

CHAPTER 11

900-Foot Jesus

"Ralph?" I asked. We were in the back of a taxi, on our way to yet another conference.

"Uh-huh," he said, barely glancing up from his Black-Berry.

"You know how when you address a crowd, and you start with an opening prayer?"

He raised an eyebrow. "Yes?"

"Well, in the prayer, you always refer to 'Him'. I was just wondering, by 'Him', do you mean Jesus, or do you mean God?" I think it's important I know who it is I am saying 'amen' to. I had been feeling guilty for weeks, worrying that I had been amen-ing to Jesus, betraying my people and, most importantly, my mother.

Ralph nodded sympathetically, an amused twinkle in his eye.

"Lisa, 'Him' always refers to God. If we're praying to Jesus, we say 'Jesus.'"

"Good to know!" Phew.

By this time, Texas Governor George W. Bush was nearing the end of his quest to become Republican nominee for president of the United States. But what the political glitterati had predicted would be a cakewalk for the Texas governor wasn't working out quite how they had expected, with Bush facing unexpectedly stiff competition from Arizona Senator John McCain, a well-regarded and highly decorated Vietnam War veteran. The quick-tongued, apparently hot-tempered Navy pilot had been shot down over Hanoi and captured by the North Vietnamese, where he spent seven grueling and brutal years as a prisoner of war. After years of beatings, he is still unable to lift both of his arms past his waist, a constant reminder of his years in the middle of that war. To the annoyance of the Bush clan, McCain had captured the hearts of many in the Republican party, and there were whispers that he might win the nomination over his rival, George W.

The battle royale began in New Hampshire on January 8, 2000, where McCain was able to pull off a surprising primary victory, soundly beating Bush by nineteen points. Team Bush knew that if McCain won the upcoming South Carolina primary on February 19 (the most important contest in the series of primary elections leading up to Super Tuesday), his momentum would be unstoppable. They called on Ralph Reed, fearless organizer, quiet rabble-rouser, and master manipulator, to help. My boss was hired, as a mail and phone campaigner, to whip the God-fearing voters of South Carolina into a pro-Bush, anti-McCain frenzy. Whip them up he did, destroying McCain's presidential hopes in a few weeks.

He sent out a blistering bugger of direct mail, nailing McCain on the issue of the Confederate flag waving over South Carolina, causing a shit-storm the size of Katrina. A sizeable faction of good ol' boys wanted to keep their Confederate flag, racist undertones be damned, despite complaints from civil rights groups who said there should be a federal law banning it. McCain had defended the flag wavers, saying he thought it was a state rights issue, not a federal issue. But Ralph's mailer suggested otherwise, painting McCain as a politically correct liberal who would let the federal government meddle in South Carolina's right to wave its damn flags. The good ol' boys were not pleased.

And, although it was never proven, there were accusations of push polling (polls designed to "push" respondents toward a negative impression of an opponent) and whisper campaigns, like the rumor that McCain's adopted Bangladeshi daughter (whose dark skin stood out against the lily-white McCain family backdrop) was actually an illegitimate love child created with a cocoa companion. This completely baseless rumor, seemingly from out of nowhere, spread like wildfire among local Godaphiles. Coupled with the Confederate flag issue, McCain's fate was sealed. He lost the votes of countless rattled ultra-cons, and when George W. Bush handily won the South Carolina primary, Ralph rejoiced in a job well done. As far as Ralph was concerned, yes, things had gotten personal—but this was politics. He did what he had to do. Bush went on to sweep Super Tuesday, and clinched the nomination.

Working for Ralph was a lot like doing the Hokey-Pokey: you start with an arm and a leg, but by the end of it, you've thrown your whole self in. I started to find myself involved in just about every facet of Ralph's life. We traveled everywhere together. We spent hours in airport waiting rooms, talking shop and dishing dirt. We sucked down stale draft beers in small town bars, waiting for connecting flights. We met for breakfast in hotel lobbies, downing microwaved biscuits and weak black coffee. Occasionally, Big Les would book us on a red-eye to wherever we needed to be. The flights were typically empty and bumpy, and Ralph, knowing my fear of flying, would leave his first-class seat to talk to me in coach and tell me not to be afraid of the turbulence.

"It's going to be okay, Lisa. And if it isn't, at least we'll go down together." And I'd laugh.

Ralph, more than Xanax or in-flight Bloody Mary's, made me feel calmer. If he said things were going to be okay, that meant things were going to be okay. He was Ralph Reed; he was too smart to be wrong. He had a PhD, was an avid reader and a published author. Under his tutelage, I was learning the persuasive power of words. He read and critiqued my press releases, my statements, my speeches, showing me how to effectively get my point across, while paying meticulous attention to detail. Ralph was turning me into a writer.

As the Republican primary rolled into the 2000 general election, Team Bush called on Ralph's Christian chops less and less, as the focus had shifted to wooing mainstream and undecided voters. With less media requests, came less work for me. That's when Ralph shifted my job focus and introduced me to campaign fund-raising. In Ralph's world, it was never good enough to merely meet any goal—you had to exceed it. His plan was to become a George W. Bush Pioneer (the highest tier of financial giver in the campaign), which required he raise $100,000 for the campaign. Ralph put me in charge of a fund-raiser featuring Oklahoma Governor Frank Keating (at the time Keating was rumored to be on the vice presidential short list) and sent me off to the Sooner State to get the party started.

"It's addictive, isn't it?" Ralph remarked as $1,000.00 checks began rolling in for the rubber chicken dinner down in Tulsa. The dinner was held on the top floor of the Oral Roberts University Prayer Tower, a 200-foot-high structure whose design elements include an observation deck meant to resemble Jesus' crown of thorns, with red accents inspired by the color of Christ's blood on the cross, with an eternal gas flame at the top. I had to take a Xanax in the elevator on the way up—along with a fear of flying, I also suffer from numbing vertigo (not to mention claustrophobia and an ungodly fear of public restrooms—but that's another story).

The man who built the tower, the late Oral Roberts, was the MC Hammer of televangelism, known for excessive accessorizing and rash financial decision-making. But while MC Hammer timed his shirtless bad self out of the music business, Roberts had staying power, or more likely, a wealthier following. "May God bless you in your bodies, in your spirits, and in your finances," was his favorite blessing. Who can forget 1987 when Roberts took to the airwaves to announce that a 900-foot-tall Jesus had appeared before him, instructing him to build a medical school? If he didn't get $8 million to build the school, that God would call him home. As a result, he got $9 million and he wasn't called home until 2009. If I remember correctly, my fifth-grade Hebrew school teacher, Morah (Hebrew for "teacher") Silverman, said that the last person that she knew of whom God had talked to was Moses. But then, what did she know?

If the skyscraper-style Prayer Tower isn't enough to entice God-fearing students to the liberal arts Christian charismatic university, there were always the pair of colossal hands clasped in prayer that shot out from the ground like Jack's beanstalk. The cupped hands were cold as a gynecologist's and big as Godzilla—at sixty feet, it is the world's largest bronze sculpture. In an abbreviated skirt and with my mouth agape, I stared up at this garish display of Godaphilia and pondered my surroundings. Can a divine being actually speak directly to man (or woman) and instruct them on what to do and how to do it? Could he be using us to carry out his orders, or are we (and by "we" I mean "them") using him to get what they want?

I scanned the ballroom that would serve as the venue for our magnificent fund-raiser. Ralph had flown in from Atlanta for a final walk-through, and he could be very particular about things. I wanted to make sure I didn't disappoint him.

"Looks good," Ralph said, looking around, the tinkling of piano keys in the background. "Oh good, you got my piano player," he said, walking toward the melody.

"What are you thinking of playing?" he asked the middle-aged lady pianist as she tinkled away.

"I will begin with 'Stars and Stripes,'" she said, her polished nails giving the keys a twirl. I grimaced. Couldn't she bust out some Elton John or something? "Then, I will rotate between 'God Bless America' and 'Proud to be an American,'" she said, striking a baritone chord.

"Perfect," Ralph said, pleased, as I tried not to roll my eyes too far back into my head.

In the elevator on our way down to sea level, Ralph asked what I thought of the entertainment.

"You know, I probably would have picked something a little more modern, song-wise. All that 'God Bless America' stuff—it's not really for me."

"None of this is for you. You are not representative of the average American."

Out of Ralph's mouth, with no warning, came this abounding, fierce, almost maniacal roar of laughter. The sound made the hairs on my arms stand up. I hadn't said anything funny, and I didn't consider what he had said all that funny. But I guess he was right. Over the past decade I hadn't come across any other trash-talking, booze-swilling, foul-mouth, fornicating Jewish mouthpieces for Christian Crusaders. My habits certainly didn't make me any less of a Republican, but perhaps they didn't make me the best person to pick out the entertainment at a George W. Bush for President fund-raiser.

"These people are going to love it," he said after a moment of quiet awkwardness. And he was right. As guests left the sold-out fund-raiser, there was no mention about the food, or the décor, but the music: Bravo!

I was glad when it was over, and not because I couldn't take one more rendition of Lee Greenwood's "Proud to be an American" on a baby grand. It was because the big praying hands sticking out of the Oklahoma dirt had begun to blend in the background of my life. The fact that this didn't bother me, that it was normal to see giant hands reaching for Jesus jettisoning out of soil, bothered me. Was I starting to lose my identity? Had I become so absorbed in my ambition that I was slowly assimilating?

Ideologically, I stuck out like a sore thumb. I am pro-choice. I believe that gay, straight, or plain confused, every person on this earth has equal value and therefore should be able to marry whomever they choose. I am Jewish, yet I was surrounded by non-Jews who, while well-meaning folks themselves, thought that while I was a very nice person, wasn't it such a shame that I would be spending all of eternity burning in hell with Ken Mehlman?

Ken Mehlman (gay and Jewish) was the former political director for George W. Bush. After coming out, Mehlman admitted his remorse over having championed laws that denied gay men and women the right to marry. Maybe me, Ken, and others like us (read: social moderates) can separate, almost compartmentalize, our private selves from our political selves in the name of our loftier goals. Personally, I considered big government a bigger evil than the ladies who stood outside abortion clinics with a stuffed baby duck in one hand and a poster of a half-aborted fetus in the other. Right or wrong, I knew that it would be near impossible for *Roe v. Wade* to be overturned (it is, by the way, a law regarding privacy more so than the result of unprotected penetration). But higher taxes would impale my paycheck, tomorrow, unless the right people are in office. This was my brain's way of justifying the paradox: I was a socially moderate Jew in a political party dominated by religious social conservatives. A pigeon among the cats, as it were.

After the fund-raiser, Ralph handed me the car keys. The ride down the road to our Oklahoma hotel was straight as an arrow. No traffic lights, only the headlights of our rental car and, every now and again, a single swinging, blinking red traffic light indicating a four-way stop. We passed streets named Jessie, Rebecca, and Mary. It was very peaceful, very safe: just us, two coworkers winding through the Oklahoma plains. Within this vehicle, wrapped in this moment, we were equals. I wasn't the underling and he wasn't the boss. He was a man named Ralph and I was a girl named Lisa; two souls in one car on different journeys. I felt brave in the intimacy.

"Oral Roberts said that God told him to build a skyscraper in the middle of Oklahoma."

"Yeah," Ralph answered.

"Do you think that's what really happened?" I asked.

"I don't know. I think some people do have that kind of relationship with God," he answered.

"Do you?" I asked.

"God told me to stop what I was doing and work with George W. Bush, and that's exactly what I'm doing."

"Are you sure God talked to you? Or would you say you had more of an instinct or a rationalization of what your subconscious is actually telling you?"

He paused, thinking about my question, and shrugged. "Maybe."

CHAPTER 12

I Am That Kind of Girl

I was relieved to learn that I am not the kind of girl who would do anything for money. Unfortunately, I had to find that out the hard way, scratch that, the semi-hard-on way.

I had been working with Ralph for over a year, and everything was going swimmingly. That must have been why he wanted to find me a husband, or at the very least, get me laid. When Christians (well-meaning, of course) act as a dating service for their ethnic friends, they consider one thing: your ethnicity. A girl Jew for a boy Jew, we'd lock together like Legos picked from the pile. Knowing this, I'm always wary of accepting a blind date, but since Ralph arranged the whole thing, I felt obligated to go. And well, a girl's gotta eat!

Jason came to Atlanta by way of private jet to take me to dinner. The founder of a nationwide chain of cell phone stores, he was rich, eligible, and, wait for it, Jewish. He was picking me up (by car) at about 7:30 P.M. Currently it's 4:30 P.M. at Century Strategies.

"I'm out of here, Big Les," I said, standing in her doorway.

"Where you going?"

"I have a meeting," I lied.

"You do not!"

"Am I the only one who works around here?" she yelled, regardless of the fact that Ralph sat busily working in his office.

I was three hours from getting lucky or disappointed. Regardless, I wasn't going down (literally or figuratively) without good hair. It would take me twenty minutes to shower and apply my makeup and every bit of the remaining two and a half hours to deal with my 'do.

Standing in my towel in front of the mirror, I wrapped my thick wavy hair around my forty-dollar round brush and wrestled with my industrial-grade blow-dryer.

With my coif finally done, my triceps burning, and a glass of wine down the hatch, I was down to makeup and wardrobe. I stood before my closet in my undergarments deliberating what to wear. I tried to keep in mind that my outfit, and quite possibly what happened on the date, might get back to Ralph, or end up again, on the front page of the *New York Times:* "Twenty-Nine-Year-Old Press Secretary to Former Christian Coalition Leader Found Nude in Ditch; Blood Alcohol Ridiculously over the Legal Limit."

I considered all the options: cleavage, or no cleavage? Did I show legs, or wear pants? After much consideration I stayed true to my inner Lisa: skintight snakeskin-patterned red dress with ankle-strapped black heels. As I buckled my patent-leather high-heeled Mary Janes, the outside buzzer of my apartment rang. I turned on the television, excitedly flipping to the twenty-four-hour channel that was the apartment's security camera. Standing by the front door, I saw all I needed to know: no chemistry. He stood about five foot nine. His physique was undefined, some might say doughy. His skin was as pallid as cold cream, and his eyes were small as a ground animal's. A closely buzzed crop of red hair circled the perimeter of his domelike head. And the ultimate bummer—the warm, damp Southern evening had taken its toll on his button-down shirt.

"Swamp stains," I sighed. "Ew."

I grabbed my bag and went to greet my "hot" date. As I approached the gate, the scent of his cologne withered my nasal hairs.

"Hi, I'm Lisa," I said, busting out my broadest fake smile. He looked me up and down.

"Wow, you're not so bad. I wasn't sure what I was going to be taking out tonight."

I knew what he meant: you just never know what you're going to get when the religious right plays matchmaker to two Jews.

As part of my personal tribute to Emily Post, I said nothing and just laughed a little laugh. I always tried to be polite the first thirty minutes of a date—at least before the cocktails started kicking in. He opened the door to his rental car, and we were off.

"Where are we going?" I asked. I hoped it would be a place with dim lighting but clearly marked exits.

"The Dining Room at the Ritz-Carlton," he answered.

It was not lost on me that I was being taken to a hotel to have dinner. I felt like a farm-fattened turkey just before Christmas.

"The Ritz! How lovely."

"Welcome to the Ritz-Carlton, ma'am. Will you be staying with us this evening?"

"No," I said. I handed the white-gloved valet attendant my freshly painted OPI "I'm Not Really a Waitress" hand.

"I have a room," Jason interjected.

We entered the dining room and were escorted to a booth tucked uncomfortably at the back of the half-empty five-star restaurant.

"So, how did you get to Atlanta?" he asked.

I instinctively went into first date automatic pilot, delivering my carefully crafted, earnest, yet sassy monologue designed to prove that yes, I was potentially wife-worthy, aka a genuine woman of substance (albeit a woman who drank a few too many bottles of wine and had a weak spot for streetwalker chic).

I talked about being the youngest person ever to work in the Arizona governor's campaign press office, how I moved to Washington, DC, despite not having a job lined up. I went so deep into my own shit that I didn't realize my wineglass had been refilled twice and from here on out the booze was doing all of the talking. I was deep into part two of my story: taking the job in New Jersey working on the reelection campaign for Governor Christine Todd Whitman.

"Whitman is a mean, mean woman," I slurred.

He stared at me blankly.

"Christie. Whitman. Blond woman. Large teeth. Looks like your sixth-grade gym teacher."

Jason interrupted, clearly bored and determined to change the subject.

"Just promise me you're not one of those Jews for Jesus freaks."

I shook my head, giggling.

Now it was his turn to talk.

He talked about his money, his business, and his airplane.

"How about we fly to the Caribbean for your birthday, Lisa?"

I giggled some more, and wondered how good of a friend was I? Could I pretend to be interested in a man for the sole purpose of getting my gal pals a free Caribbean vacation on a private jet? The jury was still out.

"I have to make a phone call, it's business," he said. "Will you join me for a second up in my room?"

Now, I have been invited up to a dorm room to see a "fish tank" and into a fraternity house to check out a "bootleg Nirvana CD," but for some reason, the ol' business call trick didn't set off the alarm bells.

"Sure," I chirped.

We got our bill, he paid our check, and I followed him over to the elevator. He pressed the button for one of the top floors and turned to me to make sure I was impressed. I checked the time—10:30 P.M. already.

"I have to be at work tomorrow, so once you are done, we should probably get going . . . if that's okay."

In his room, I waited patiently for Jason to finish his business. With his cell phone up to his ear, he turned to me and held up one finger indicating he would be just a minute.

"No problem," I mouthed, pretending to be enthralled with the room service menu. If I squinted hard enough I could make out the words.

"Voice mail," he whispered.

"Hey, Jack, it's Jason, I'm in Atlanta, call me when you can." He flipped his phone closed and returned it to the top of the black leather desk.

"Do you know Jack Abramoff?" he asked.

"Ralph's friend?"

"Yeah."

Ralph often talked about his old buddy Jack Abramoff, whose couch he crashed on back when they were young Republican organizers fresh out of college. He had introduced Jack to his wife, and the two men were still very close, from what I could gather.

"I know who he is, but I have never met him."

"We are buying a casino together, and the deal is just about to go through."

"Casino? Sounds cool!" I said, trying not to feel nauseous as the carpeted floor spun in front of me. As I perched on the edge of his king-sized bed, I could feel the wine from dinner gurgling in my belly.

"Do you think I can get some water?" I asked, trying to maintain composure.

"Yeah, help yourself," he said, pointing to the nine-dollar bottle of spring water. "I gotta hit the bathroom, be right back."

I sipped my water and encouraged sobriety to arrive sooner rather than later.

I heard the bathroom door open and turned around. Silly me, I thought he had gone into the bathroom to pee. Actually, he had gone to the john to slip into something more comfortable: his birthday suit.

As he emerged and made his way over to me, my vision suddenly returned and I saw Jason's one-eyed flesh pistol bobbing in my direction, at a sorry half-mast. Ladies and gentlemen, there is nothing quite like a full frontal assault to sober you up.

"What are you doing?" I squealed, his ball sack approaching me at a very alarming rate of speed.

"Let's cut to the chase," he murmured, moving in for a kiss.

I let him slobber all over my face for a few seconds (I am a lady, after all), and if I remember correctly, I think he copped a handful of my left boob. If this had happened to me today, I would have gotten up and thought nothing of using my three-inch spiked heel to puncture each sack. Back then, the only thing I could think of was, *How can I not have sex without embarrassing Ralph?*

LIFE OF THE PARTY

I chose to play the pass-out game. The pass-out game traces its origins back to the popular pastime of playing possum. It happens to be one of my favorites. You lie there like you are dead (or passed out) until the enemy either moves on or, in my case, falls into a deep, deep sleep. Then you throw his (or her, depending on what type of encounter you are looking to escape) arm off of you, grab your clothes as quickly as you can from off of the floor, put them on, and tiptoe toward the door. Then you run like the motherfucking wind.

Like a diver running low on oxygen, I gasped for air.

"Are you okay?" he asked.

What do you mean, am I okay? No, you fat, filthy fucknugget, I'm not fucking okay. You just came out of the bathroom waving your wiener-worm in my face without any foreplay, advance notice, or for that matter, an invitation. It's the year 2000, turd burglar—just because you picked up the check, doesn't mean I have to pick up your penis.

That is what I wanted to say.

"Oh, I'm not feeling well . . . I need more water and then probably just to rest a minute," is what I said. I grabbed the water again, took a swill, and then lay back down on the bed, closed my eyes, and feigned death.

After an hour of playing possum, I removed his hairy blond arm from my waist and then waited to see if he stirred. I placed my left foot on the floor first . . . then the right. I waited a few more seconds until I heard him return to snoring. I grabbed my purse, my phone, and sprinted on my tiptoes for the door. Freedom was mine.

"I need a cab, please," I said to the doorman downstairs, panting and quasi-hysterical with relief.

"No problem, my lady," he said, a Caribbean twill in his voice.

Lisa Baron

It was 3:30 A.M. I lit a cigarette and tried to calm down as I waited for my lift home.

"Your cab, Ma'am," he said, his white-gloved hand opening the door.

"I'm not a prostitute, you know," I blurted.

I wasn't sure which one of us I was trying to convince.

Chapter 13

Pantily Clad

I showed up to work feeling like ten pounds of hammered shit stuffed in a five-pound bag—this was to be the mother of all hangovers. I prayed it would be one of those quiet days where the toughest choice I faced would be whether to order a size six or an eight while online shopping. Then I would e-mail all of my friends, take a two-hour lunch, and leave by four.

"Girl, you are not looking fabulous," Amanda said from her beige cubby adorned with glossy magazine cutouts of Madonna. Amanda was a superhero in girl-next-door clothing, an ultra-capable brunette sweetie-pie, who happened to be Republican Party royalty. Her grandmother was the Republican National Party co-chairman during the historic Republican takeover of Congress during the Clinton years. Amanda hailed from Mississippi, was curiously obsessed with Madonna, and owned a wiener dog, Briggs, that she named after her previous boss. She had short brown hair, drove a red Ford Escort, and described Ralph as a koala bear: he looks cute and cuddly, she warned, but if you get too close he will claw your face off.

"I can always tell when she is hung over," Emily chimed in. "Hair in a low wet bun, no makeup, oversized black sunglasses, and a venti Starbucks equals hung over."

Emily was a twenty-two-year-old precocious blonde with a furious work ethic and an attitude to match. She was from Cumming, Georgia (made famous by the standoff that never took place between the Ku Klux Klan and Oprah Winfrey), was up for any task, and often outperformed the management she was taking orders from. She drove a white SUV we called the Honky and became infuriated every time Ralph walked by her desk and stole one of her newspapers.

"Last night—you guys wouldn't believe it if I told you," I said.

"We believe you. Now talk," Amanda encouraged (she was always encouraging me).

"Ralph set me up on a blind date last night."

"That is not good," she said, suppressing a smile.

"As you guys know," I said, addressing both girls, "being whored out, by anyone, even Ralph, isn't really an issue for me. I did, however, take exception to my date accosting me with his pale, circumcised" (a hint of gratitude) "penis."

Then I launched into the whole sorry tale.

"So, not a love connection," Amanda reasoned.

"Not a love connection," I soberly confirmed.

"Too bad you didn't barf on him," added Emily.

Emily and Amanda were stationed in the block of cubicles they named Cubbyland. The four of us, Big Les, and Ralph's business partner, Tim Phillips (who often worked from home), were the political arm of Century Strategies. Tim was a very ordinary, very tall, very de-voted family man—maybe not the brain trust one might assume helped Ralph turn a small business into a multimillion-dollar empire.

While I would've loved to have stuck around and continued to enter-tain Emily and Amanda, my hangover headache needed immediate at-tention. I left the girls hunched over their desks laughing and continued my pathetic trudge down the hallway to my office, making a quick pit stop into the company break room. The Century Strategies break room doubled as a kitchen and a full-service hair salon, and it was not unusual to waltz in on any given Wednesday around 4:00 P.M. and find Tim in a smock, sitting in front of a large, propped-up, full-sized mirror receiving hair color from Theresa the hairdresser. Theresa cruised through the office once a month with a caboodle full of scissors, smocks, and hair color. She owned her own shop, but had worked out a deal with Ralph to come in once a month to manage his mane as well as the tresses of his entire family, Tim's entire family, and any employee of Cen Strat who didn't mind a little hair color dripping into their eye while they fired off an e-mail.

Praise the Lord, there was no coiffing taking place this morning—the pungent smell from the pigment would've sent me running to the bath-room. The break room, when not a beauty parlor, contained a well-stocked cornucopia of junk food that ranged from Famous Amos Chocolate Chip Cookies, Oreos (regular and double-stuffed), Twinkies, cartons of king-sized Twix bars, variety packs of potato chips (if you consider Cheetos a chip), and a stocked bar of sodas. I grabbed two bags of Doritos, Oreos, one bottled water, a two-pack of chocolate pudding, and a Dr Pepper. I set my stash on my desk, placed my laptop into its docking station, and waited for everything to connect—including my brain.

I could hear Big Les gabbing fast and loud from across the hall. When you are born and raised in the South, the English language is virtually unintelligible at that rate of speed. It was like white noise filling my numbed-out head. This explains why I didn't hear the footsteps that had entered my office.

"So, how did it go?" Ralph said, standing behind me.

I quickly minimized my computer screen and swung my chair around, quick enough to send my stomach flying into my throat.

"How did what go?" I said, pretending to be professional while squeezing out a smile.

"Last night, didn't you go out with Jason?" he asked.

"Oh yes, yes, that. It was very fine," I said.

"So glad. He's staying at the Ritz, I believe, perhaps we can meet him for drinks before he leaves."

He turned to leave and then stopped in my doorway, his gaze locking on the carpet.

"What's this?" Ralph asked.

"What's what?"

There was a scene unfolding right outside of my office, and would command my fullest attention. This was rare—normally I was far too self-absorbed to notice what was happening in the corridors of Century Strategies. The week before, for instance, Amanda said she had seen a geriatric black man walking around the office with a cane. "Did you see the office creeper?" she said excitedly. The news of this octogenarian drifter did little to pull me away from my e-mails and Snickers bar. (A building-wide notice was subsequently distributed to all of the suite holders confirming that a man with a cane was going around offices stealing laptops.)

Outside my doorway, I saw Ralph begin to bend down to pick up what looked like a bright white egg in a nest of black. Due to the mental haze associated with my hangover, it took me a minute to focus in on the roadkill sprawled out in my place of work. Then I recognized it immediately as the crotch of my opaque black tights, custom-made to hold your butt in and smooth over panty lines!

Once I made this positive ID, my body began moving in slow motion. "NOOOOOOOOO!" I yelled, my arms in the air. Ralph's head started to turn, his expression one of sheer confusion. I leapt out of my chair and instinctively dove, face-first, to capture them, and felt my knuckles graze Ralph's as I yanked my unmentionables from the Right Hand of God.

My knees burned with hot flecks of industrial-grade carpet, and I opened my eyes slowly. With the anticipation of any outfielder who didn't yet know if she had caught the fly ball, I, little by little, finger by finger, opened my hand to see if, in fact, I had captured my hosiery. My heart started pumping blood again—they were in my grasp.

I immediately and instinctively blamed Big Les.

"Leslie,"—I referred to her by her given name in front of Ralph—"are these yours?" I asked, shaking them above my head, in my most headmistressy voice.

Ralph seemed confused. "Are your knees okay, Lisa?" I nodded bravely, and he went into his office and closed the door.

Amanda and Emily ran out from Cubbyland to see what all the commotion was about. Emily plucked them out of my hand. "They are a size small, the tag says Express, and *these* are *yours*, Lisa!" Emily said.

"No, they are not," I insisted loudly, hoping Ralph could hear through his thick wood door. "How would my shapewear show up at the office?"

"I do not shop at that store, and I do not wear a size small," Big Les bellowed.

"They aren't mine," said Amanda. "I am from Mississippi, and we do not wear panties like that." (She was always using Mississippi as an excuse.)

The sad truth is, they were, of course, mine. When I had gotten dressed that morning, I must have accidentally picked my outfit out of the laundry pile. Unbeknownst to me, my enterprising undergarments had been clinging to the side of my pant leg, hitching a ride all the way to Century Strategies before parachuting gently down in the hallway, in the direct path of Ralph Reed.

Mad as I was at my tights, I was thankful to them for creating a bigger talking point than my horrific date the night before. Presumably in shock at the sight of me holding my hosiery in the air, Ralph forgot to bring up my date—and any future dates—with the wiener waver. My knickers had provided an excellent diversion, a crucial strategy in politics. What I lacked in academic excellence, I made up for in my unsurpassed talent for turning hangovers into valuable life lessons.

Chapter 14

Thank You, Sir, May I Have Another?

I knew you needed seven years drug-free to earn top White House Secret Service clearance. I wasn't clear, however, what the policy was regarding double-platinum membership to a hard-core gay porn website. The person who stole my credit card number (these days we call it identity theft) could have just bought a stereo or television like a normal criminal, but he (or perhaps she) had an itch that needed scratching, and they used my card to do the dirty work. I was in the middle of dealing with this debacle when Big Les asked me if I had a preference for when I would like to fly out to Austin, Texas, for general election night 2000. With all the work I had done for Bush, Ralph was rewarding me by inviting me to what we hoped would be the biggest party in Republican America. I was overjoyed. "Thank God you're going," Amanda said. "If he left you behind, you would probably fly into some sort of fit of separation anxiety and pee on his office carpet and chew up the papers on his desk like a panic-stricken puppy." Which was true. All worries about my credit card being used to purchase man-on-man-on-woman-on-man action dissolved and I promised myself I would deal with the bank later—I had some packing to do!

It was starting to feel like the pieces of my plan were coming together. Glancing in the rearview mirror of my political career, I looked back on all the grunt work I had done—I had written the stump speeches, driven the parade routes on Saturdays and Sundays, eaten corn dogs and tater tots, started smoking again, toured Middle America in an RV, and spent far too long engaged in meaningless conversation with zealots and sycophants, nodding my head while wondering what I should have for dinner. Now I was going to (hopefully) be partying with the new president of the United States.

Ralph knew that even though I was happy at Century Strategies, my ultimate goal was to work in a Republican White House administration in Washington, DC. It may seem cold that I was so willing to jump ship to ride a better vessel, but that's how you play the game. You scratch my back, I'll scratch yours. I wanted to go to the White House—Ralph could help me with that—and he wanted to soften up his image and move from the far right to the political center, which was where I came in. I was picky about what television and radio opportunities Ralph did, only agreeing to those with topics on politics or the presidential race. Seeing as Ralph had spent a lifetime earning a reputation as a missing link in the holy Trinity, it was going to be a delicate, long-term endeavor, rebranding the firebrand.

Any time I received a request for Ralph to appear on a political talking-head show, I was to clear it through the Bush for President press office. A cute little press tart with a hint of sugar in her voice would say, "Well, we think United States Senator Olympia Snowe is a better representative right now," or, "We are waiting to hear if Pennsylvania Governor Tom Ridge is available. Do you mind declining?" I could hear her batting eyelashes through the phone. Like grunge music and *Beverly Hills, 90210*, it seemed like Godaphiles were out of style in the year 2000. The Bush press tart who was assigned to the South never directly came out and said that we weren't good for their image, but the message we received was loud and clear: Ralph represented the hard right and Bush was working hard to brand himself as a "Compassionate Conservative." (Fast-forward to the Bush reelection in 2004, when his support from the right was waning—that's when it became politically expedient for Bush to name Ralph Southeastern chairman of his reelection campaign.)

I threw some clothes and my hair dryer in my carry-on baggage and hopped a plane to the capital of the Lone Star State the day before the voters of the United States of America would choose their next president. Ralph and I landed at Austin's International Airport and hailed a cab directly to the Bush for President National Headquarters. As soon as we arrived, Ralph disappeared with Bush Campaign Chief Karl Rove—a close friend of his—and I wandered the halls talking and visiting with staffers whom I knew from campaigns and administrations past. The world of political campaign consultants, operatives, and otherwise is smaller than you might think. I saw some old buddies from my Dole for President days, a couple of pals from the gubernatorial race I worked on in Iowa, and a friend from the United States senatorial race in California, and hoped I wouldn't bump into Ari. When people asked me what I was up to these days, I told them about Ralph. This generally resulted in a long pause followed by a head twist similar to the way Nipper, the RCA dog, reacted to hearing music come from the Victor voice-recording machine: with dubious wonderment.

"I know," I told them. "It's weird, but it works."

Election Day is always an anxious, stomach-churning, hand-wringing, did-I-do-everything-I-could've-done type of day—and this one more than most. We knew Bush had a good chance of winning, but we were nervous because Al Gore had leaked the police report about George Bush getting a DUI just days before. Even Ralph seemed worried about the damage this would cause. We knew that it was going to be a close call, and there was no telling if the night was going to end in triumph or tears.

Back in my campaign days on the road, you could always tell if I was employed or unemployed by the contents of my wash bag. If I had designer-brand shampoos and conditioners lined up in the shower, I was employed. Unemployment meant lathering up in one of the poor man's imposter shampoos. I always dreaded those trips down the beauty aisle, where I'd pass the Bed Head, Nexxus, and Phyto with a heavy heart and a light wallet, and drag myself over to the shampoos-and-conditioners-that-suck section. While I was still desperate to make my dreams come true, at least it wouldn't be the end of my world if Bush didn't win. I had a job with Ralph, and a steady supply of Aveda shampoo and conditioner. This was a refreshing change of pace for me, switching from Pantene to Aveda, knowing my life didn't hang in the balance depending on the outcome of the night's count.

I attended a late afternoon Bush for President Get-Out-the-Vote rally in a hangar at the local private airport. I stood on the edge of what felt like a sea of conservative plankton, waving my "I Love Bush" homemade sign, whooping and hollering for the governor and First Lady Laura Bush. It always struck me as bizarre that people would ever choose to show up for a political rally. I mean—had this not been the manner in which I paid my rent and supported my shopping habit, I surely could think of about a hundred other places I'd rather be than at a rally . . . like at home in bed or at Nordstrom's. I looked around me and saw thousands of what Ralph called "true believers." Half of them had never met Bush, and had only seen him on television or caught a campaign commercial here or there, but they still longed for him to hold their babies, sign their T-shirts, and shake their hands. They wanted him to be their leader—to take their fight for their constitutional rights to Washington, DC. It was hard not to get swept up in their pure idealism.

Eventually, I made my way back to the main hotel where most of the out-of-towners associated with the campaign were staying. The lobby was packed, swarming with anxious supporters chitchatting, breaking only briefly to take a swill of their drink of choice. I found Ralph sitting with his wife and my old buddy, *Crisis* magazine editor Deal Hudson. I took drink orders for everyone—nothing for Ralph, and a vodka for Hudson. God bless the Catholics, you can always count on them for happy hour.

The bar was three people thick. It took me thirty minutes to order the drinks.

"What'll you have?" the hotel bartender said, pointing at me.

"Grey Goose and grapefruit, please."

There is something very "tropical shirts and bad-dancing" about ordering a named cocktail. It's almost like you're not serious about what you are about to drink.

Similarly, I think hopping aboard a bar stool in your miniskirt and Manolo Blahniks to order a Cosmopolitan is equally ridiculous. You're not Carrie, and I'm not Samantha.

"A Greyhound?" he said.

"Sort of," I said, "with a splash of tonic. And if you don't have yellow grapefruit—meaning, if you only have pink—I'll have something else."

"We have yellow." He winked.

Not feeling like standing in this line again anytime soon, I yelled over a cowboy hat, that had moved in my way, "Make mine a double!"

I took my "this is not a Greyhound" and headed back over to Ralph. I handed Deal his drink and slurped up my cocktail as we talked about the latest election developments.

I went back to the bar and ordered another double. And another. And then another two. I consumed five doubles in under two hours. I weigh 130 pounds.

The next thing I know, I'm in a bright red, plastic hooded poncho with a blue plastic cup full of beer trying to stay dry under the drizzling Texas sky. You wouldn't have known by looking at me whether I was at a national election night gathering waiting to find out who the next leader of the free world would be, or a tailgate party. I remember seeing a big stage where, if all went well, the president-elect would deliver his acceptance speech; rows and rows of bleachers filled with camera crews from around the world; throngs of people; and, on the outskirts of the stadium, a dozen or so trailers. Weaving in and out of the large outdoor crowd, I ran into one of my old Dole for President buddies.

"Lisa, want to see something awesome?" he asked me.

"Um, yez, please," I said, excited while also trying to focus.

"Follow me," he said, leading me through the heavy crowd toward the white trailers. Some were being used by the news media to house their election night coverage crews. Some trailers were for VIPs.

"Don't say a word," my buddy instructed as he opened the door to the trailer marked "Private."

I nodded in agreement and put my finger to my mouth to show I was serious.

Not talking was not going to be a problem. It was all I could do to keep the world from spinning out from under me, and I needed every able brain cell to walk a straight line and understand English. Fortunately, I had enough brain power left to make a positive ID of who was sitting in the trailer I had just entered: Wayne Newton and Bo Derek.

Beauty was not lost in translation from the big screen to real life when it came to Bo Derek. She was breathtaking. In my drunken lust, I imagined her in braids and a bikini running down the beach toward Dudley Moore in the movie *10*. Her eyes were perfectly almond-shaped, and her hair looked like spun gold. She was slim and sat quietly at the end of a padded bench closest to the television that was tuned in to the election results on CNN. Even through my beer goggles, it was clear that Wayne Newton was no stranger to the plastic surgeon's office. He had a full head of midnight-black hair and an orange hue to his lifted face. He wore a thick leather jacket bedazzled with crystals and letters. No one looked up at us as we took seats directly behind Wayne. I tried to use Wayne Newton's young wife's human-head-sized diamond to focus and catch my breath. But it was too late. My stomach began to turn, and my head became dizzy. I wished the wave of nausea away, but like a psycho ex-boyfriend, it wouldn't leave me alone. The trailer started to spin, like Dorothy's house in *The Wizard of Oz*, and Bo Derek's ethereal beauty faded into fuzz.

"Please don't throw up, please don't throw up," I pleaded with myself, staggering over to the kitchen sink and plucking a bottled water out of a bowl of ice. I sipped my water and tried to use the power of suggestion to stop my insides from introducing themselves to Wayne and Bo. I believed that all I needed to make it over this hump was some cold water on the face and a firm talking to myself, from myself. I counted to three (in my head, of course) and motioned to my friend that I was going to check out the back of the medium-sized trailer. It had no walls, only paper thin doors that divided up space. I dove into the bathroom, which was a tad bit bigger than that of an airplane: but at least on an airplane, the roar of the jet engines drown out any sort of background noise. I splashed cold water on my face a half dozen times all the while looking in the mirror chanting the following phrase, "you will not throw up, you are fine, you will not throw up, you are fine." I paused a couple of times to figure out if I was in the middle of a dream or if I was really this wasted in a Texas trailer with Mr. Las Vegas and a 1970s sex kitten. I begged with my reflection, "Lisa Gimbel, do not embarrass us [I have no idea who the "us" was—Ralph? My family?] by puking in this pea-sized trailer, you are better than this."

But I wasn't. I was sick. I had seconds to find a place to dispose of the vomit that was in my throat. I crouched down in front of the plastic toilet. In an attempt at covering the heaving and gagging noise I was about to make, I gave the courtesy flush. But no water flowed. The fucking thing was waterless. I guess they didn't want Bo Derek, or anyone for that matter, dropping any deuces. That's fine, but how was I to flush down hunks of bar pretzels and grapefruit juice and vodka with no water. That's when I saw it, the shower!!!!!! Not two seconds into my test run on the shower did I violently spew chucks. The shower worked! The vodka and grapefruit burned my throat and the pretzels were just as disgusting coming up as they were going down. After what seemed like eternity, I ran the shower to cover the crime scene.

Once I was satisfied I washed it all away, I returned to my spot at the sink, splashed some more water on my face and reassured myself all would be okay.

I opened the bathroom door to find Wayne, Wayne's wife, some random person, another random person and Bo Derek staring blankly at me.

My friend mouthed, *"What the fuck?"*

I waved and ran out of the trailer back into the rain, as fast as I could. "Thanks for the water!" I yelled.

I spent the rest of the night crouched behind walls in my red plastic poncho, hiding from Ralph, knowing there was no way I would be able to pretend I was sober. This election night felt like it was lasting forever, and in a way, it did.

CHAPTER 15

Death by a
Thousand Douchebags

The election didn't end that night. Nor the next night, nor the next, nor the next. When it did end, three months later in Florida, my hangover was long gone. But the country's recovery was just beginning. Brief history lesson: The United States elects a president based on an electoral college system. This (what many consider arcane) system stipulates that "electors" cast votes on behalf of their state. So it is the electoral college, not actually the majority of nationwide votes, that elects the president and vice president. The larger states, like California, Texas, and Florida, have more electors than the smaller states, like Wyoming, Delaware, and North Dakota. This is why a candidate can win the popular vote of the country (see Al Gore) but lose the election on account of not winning the electoral votes from a big state. Al Gore had won the popular vote but still needed Florida's twenty-five electoral college votes to become president. So did Bush. With the results unclear, the nation stood by breathless while the Sunshine State counted ballots, one by one.

While waiting for the outcome, we tried our best to diffuse the tension at Century Strategies.

Amanda and Emily, for instance, had recently been asked to type up a memo detailing how they spent their workdays. Here is what they came up with:

> 8:30 A.M.: Debrief each other on what we did during
> the time we left work at 6:30 P.M. last night
> 9:30–10:00 A.M.: Go to break room for a snack
> 10:15 A.M.: Bathroom break
> 11:00 A.M.: Discuss what we think we might want for
> lunch
> 11:30 A.M.: Make two work-related calls
> 11:45 A.M.: Talk about Madonna (that was Amanda's
> contribution)
> Noon: Go to lunch

Ah, lunch. Lunch was our special time. Some days we brown-bagged it and jazzed up our turkey sandwiches with the vast array of sweet and salty stock the office cupboards offered. On those days, we sat around the picnic-style table with Big Les, who had the phones forwarded to the lunchroom in case Ralph called, and listened to her talk about her ex-husband, her ex-mother-in-law (whom she was still close with), her kids, and her latest attempt to lose weight. The fun was temporarily put on hold one afternoon, when Amanda reached in the fridge and came upon a Ziploc bag sloshing around with blood—dog blood. Another office worker, who was very passionate about rescuing St. Bernards, was storing a rather large blood sample that she was going to have tested for parvo. Amanda screamed, and Emily and I came running to the icebox that was being used as some sort of veterinarian test tube. "What the fuck is that?" cried Emily. I also took issue with my caramel and vanilla-swirl pudding resting on a shelf with a container of doggy funk.

And if nothing like a bloody sample showed up in the fridge, we'd waste the lunch hours at the mall across the street from our offices. It turned out to be a great economic decision for us. We spent the first hour of our lunches chasing down any mall person we saw holding a clipboard. A clipboard meant that there was a research study for a new emerging product about to be marketed to the public. If you let them take you to a back room in the mall (I know, usually you don't want anyone taking you to the back room of a mall), they show you a video, ask you a few questions, and give you fifteen bucks for your time. Sometimes twenty. The last focus group I remember attending was for a line of environmentally friendly household cleaning products. I expressed a clear disdain for what I considered a "weak and touchy-feely" alternative to the hard-core chemicals I required to clean my kitchen and bathroom. As it turned out, organic cleaning products and this business of saving the planet and going green became a multibillion-dollar industry. But like Ralph pointed out, I don't reflect the thoughts and concerns of the traditional American.

Finally, in January 2001, The Supreme Court of the United States declared George W. Bush the winner, setting the Century Strategies office abuzz with energy. We watched the Supreme Court's decision announced on TV and cheered with joy, our collective relief that the decision had gone our way palpable in the air. Afterward, we went for drinks, aware that things were about to get very interesting for all of us, especially Ralph. We had no idea quite how interesting.

First things first—Ralph sent me to Washington, DC, to work on the inauguration committee for the forty-third president of the United States, a "dream come true" moment for Lisa Gimbel, press tart. Ordered to pack two months' worth of clothes and make myself useful in DC, I found myself back on the road again. This time, I relished the fact that there were just a couple of degrees of separation between little ol' me and Mr. President himself. I stuffed as many designer dresses in my bags as possible, imagining the glamorous, high-powered gatherings I would be attending, and felt a profound sense of gratitude toward Ralph. He had taken a chance on me—a wild, reckless fornicator, a Press Tart with a Heart; and now he had been gracious enough to share the spoils of victory with me. Ralph was my teacher, protector, and high school crush rolled into one, and as such, I was filled with an odd sense of anxiety— was I really going to leave him and my family at Century Strategies for two whole months?

"Don't be silly, Lisa," I chided myself. "This is what you've been working for all these years. Don't lose sight of the bigger goal."

I took comfort in the fact that finally, with Bush's victory, my parents were happy about the path their daughter was on. Even my mother had learned to like Ralph, probably with a little help from my father, who had taken to snail-mailing me newspaper articles from the *Wall Street Journal* that quoted or referenced Ralph. These days, my mom, when asked, "So, what's Lisa up to?" was actually giving friends and family the real answer, and saying she admired me for carving my own identity and career. Working for Ralph Reed and being a Republican wasn't a point of contention anymore; it was bragging rights for my proud parents.

I returned to DC in the middle of a freezing winter, and looked around the city I knew and loved. I rode the Metro to my new digs—a hotel room in Alexandria, Virginia, where I would be spending the next two months with a roommate I had never met before. The inaugural headquarters were located inside a vacant government administration office in DC, a forty-five-minute commute from the hotel. I was finally closer both geographically and professionally to the Lincoln Bedroom than I had ever been before. I imagined my life in Washington, DC, would be extraordinary and intellectually glamorous. I couldn't wait to attend dinner parties with thought leaders, political leaders, and PhDs, where the soup du jour would be as rich as the discussion. I hoped I'd sit next to journalist, author, and speaker Thomas Friedman and he would engage me in conversation, and not just any conversation, but conversations I could understand! I was afloat with fantasies of the long walks I would take through the city where the most meaningful and empowering language wrapped around the staid old buildings. I'd slip into art museums and the Smithsonian on my lunch break and meet colleagues for drinks at the Four Seasons in Georgetown and laugh over public policy.

Reality was very different. Inside the inaugural headquarters, I roamed the halls, aimlessly, the cold daylight illuminating a kind of soulless high-level bureaucracy I had never experienced before. *So this* I thought, *is the machine.* There seemed very little for me to do. I had no set mission other than to "help out." I was just another number, a fly flocking to the sticky-sweet tape of political victory. At night I lay awake in the hotel, listening to the soft breathing of my roommate and wondering how everyone was doing back in Atlanta. My roommate and I didn't really spend much time getting to know each other, as we kept different schedules. In fact, I don't think I even remember her name. (When she left, she neglected to pay her parking bill, which was charged to my credit card—but I didn't bother to chase her down on it because I didn't know where to find her. That's how close we were.)

So focused had I been on the road ahead, I hadn't stopped to really look at the inhabitants of my destination: douchebags! I don't mean literally bags of feminine cleaning fluid; Washington to me was death by a thousand douchebags. Our nation's capital is a parallel universe where men are measured by the size of their lapel pins and where self-worth is based on for whom you work, not who you are. It's survival of the trickiest in a political jungle where self-promotion reigns supreme. Nora Ephron was exactly right (as always) when she wrote in *I Remember Nothing*, ". . . people in Washington don't talk about anyone who doesn't live in Washington, and that's the truth." It is the truth and that's what is most troublesome. Laws should be enacted here, not made here because what was happening in this microcosm of egos and bad comb-overs was not representative of what was happening in the real America. Plus, I was getting more and more skeeved out by the amount of men I saw wearing bow ties, which in my opinion, weren't as much a fashion statement as a red flag. It was to the geek what Mohawks are to the punk—overkill.

Back in Atlanta, I was somebody. In DC, I was just another skirt on the ladder, clinging on for dear life. I observed the "successful" people around me, and realized the cost at which their success had come. They had no lives. Many of them had no real relationships. They had sacrificed personal fulfillment in order to achieve their professional goals. Was this what I wanted? After coming up with my life plan in a mail room in Arizona, my values and goals had changed. Slowly but surely, I started feeling how I'd felt back in Tallahassee. I had no real sense of connection with my coworkers, something I had become used to from other campaigns and from Ralph's office. Conversations would begin and end with, "So who do you work for?" And even though my response nearly always elicited an interested response, it didn't stop me from feeling like I was associating with a bunch of social-climbing losers. I looked around and saw the system for what it really was—kids from Ivy League schools, some lacking Ivy League minds, getting promotions based on their credentials and Daddy's connections. I saw how life unfolded for the others, the hardworking careerists—they would ride the political gravy train as long as they could before becoming a lobbyist for something they could care less about, driven by paychecks and expense accounts and pensions until they were, inevitably, chewed up and spat out. If I wanted in, this was what the next ten to twelve years of my life would look like. Suddenly, Catholic luncheons and gigantic bronze hands clasped in prayer didn't seem like such a bad deal after all.

I missed Big Les. I missed Emily and Amanda. I missed Cubbyland. Most of all, I missed Ralph. I missed home. Not Arizona home, Atlanta home. I reminisced about some of my favorite moments at Century Strategies: how I would come in after a hot date, get on all fours in front of Big Les, and say, "This is what I was doing last night, Big Les." How Amanda came in to work one morning and made the toaster catch on fire. How Big Les's shih tzu got stuck in the elevators. These were the memories that comforted me.

Two months later, when Ralph, his wife, and the Cen Strat girls arrived in DC for the inauguration, I could barely conceal my excitement. The second they arrived, I checked out of the Embassy Suites in Alexandria, Virginia, bade farewell to my mirthless roomie, and checked in to the Mayflower Hotel in Washington, DC, where Big Les, Emily, Amanda, and I shared a room right next door to Ralph and JoAnne. And only then did I finally start experiencing DC in the way I had hoped I would—by partying it up.

We went to countless exclusive dinners and glittering functions, and at the end of every night I unhinged my party dress, took a swill of red wine, and collapsed on the bed butt-naked next to a sleeping Emily. A practice she did not appreciate. We watched the inaugural parade from the balcony of Bob Novak's Pennsylvania Avenue condominium, the girls and I disappearing into rooms because we thought it was cool to look around the inner sanctum of Bob Novak's apartment. As we moved about the city, people screamed and shouted out with glee, "Ralph Reed!" and then whistled and clapped. Some screamed out for auto-graphs; others just wanted to touch his hand or a piece of his clothing. It was like walking around with a member of The Beatles. I loved being in the middle of something big, and the biggest thing in my life was Ralph. Without him, I was nobody.

Chapter 16

Super Tramp

Trying to get Big Les laid was hard work. Especially considering that since Bush had become president, business at Century Strategies had increased tenfold. Conspiring to get a middle-aged woman penetrated while booking Ralph on talking-head cable shows, servicing my share of corporate clients, and pushing through the occasional hangover was, at best, daunting. Luckily, I wasn't the only one who felt that our sister in arms could use a full release. Les's friends threw her a fiftieth birthday party at which she was presented with a stripper dressed like a police officer and a Jack Rabbit vibrator. The stripper was what you might expect: an overtanned, lubed-out, balding twentysomething with a pair of handcuffs and a boom box who, after you stuff a few sweaty one dollar bills in his thong, goes home. The Jack Rabbit, well that my friends is man's, scratch that, woman's best friend. And a gift the keeps on giving.

Inspired by the thought of Big Les being dry-humped by a stripper, I came up with an idea for even more fun.

"Big Les," I said, perching on the side of her desk while she replied to e-mails. "What would you say if I offered to pay your rent for one month if all you had to do was one tiny little thing that would only take about two minutes?"

"What are you up to?" she asked, turning around in her chair and facing me.

"Come with me."

We walked to the conference room, where Emily and Amanda were waiting for us.

It was around this time that Molly Shannon was playing a spry fifty-year-old on *Saturday Night Live*. The character's name was Sally O'Malley, and she had a penchant for polyester, panty panels, and camel toes. Like Billy Crystal's Fernando Lamas and Dana Carvey's Church Lady, Sally O'Malley had become a staple on the classic comedy show, and was regularly replayed on the television in the Century Strategies conference room. We considered Sally O'Malley especially hilarious because our Southern fried soul sister—Big Les—resided in our midst.

Big Les removed a tucked-in chair from around the oval table and took a seat.

"Cue the tape," I said, pointing at the VHS player that played our favorite shows over and over. Amanda pressed PLAY.

Sally O'Malley came on the screen, her ear-length brown hair teased up in a disorderly bouffant. She was wearing a Santa Claus–style two-piece polyester jumpsuit with a wide snow-white waistband and a garnish of ruffles. With an unusually high energy level, she bounded onto the screen. "Ladies and gentlemen, my name is Sally O'Malley, and I'm proud to say I'm fifty years old. I am not one of those gals who's afraid to say her age." And then, "I like to kiiccck" (she kicked her left leg out violently, like a Rockette on crack), "sttreeetch" (entering a squatlike pose), "and *kick*!" she says, ending the calisthenics with an awkward flourish.

Trying my best to keep a straight face, I turned to Big Les with my proposition.

"I will pay your first month's rent, if you go, uninvited, into Ralph's office, stand right in front of his desk, and say, 'Ladies and gentlemen, my name is Leslie Few, and I like to kick, stretch, and kick because I'm fifty, Five-O.'"

"Are you crazy?" she said, half-laughing and half-wanting to know.

"No, I'll pay you, but you actually have to kick, stretch, and kick. You don't have to show him your camel toe."

"I am not going into Ralph Reed's office to kick and whatever else you're talking about," she said, muttering, "Some chamomile toe . . ."

"Okay, two months' rent!" I exclaimed, like I was a real auctioneer, all the while secretly hoping she didn't agree because I couldn't afford two months of her rent and mine.

It may seem as though we were being mean to Big Les, a lovely fifty-year-old woman with a heart as massive as Ralph's ego, who really did answer to her name, Big Les. Yes, we were trying to get a laugh at her expense, because for some reason we thought it would be hilarious to see Big Les kick and stretch in front of a stoic Ralph, sitting behind his throne of a desk, wearing a headset and contemplating where his next million would come from. But that's what life was like at Century Strategies in those days. Emily, Amanda, and I were like sorority sisters, pleading with Ralph's half-century assistant to come down to our twelve-year-old level, all while making a multi-million dollar company hum.

While Amanda was kicking, I was stretching and Emily was pretending to display an imaginary camel-toe, Ralph's business partner, Tim, appeared at the glass door.

"I need to see you, you, and you," he said pointing at Emily, Amanda, and me. Big Les retrieved her reading glasses from the table's tip, shook her head, and went back to her office.

Tim was a tall thin man in his late thirties with graying hair, which explained why he was a regular in the once-monthly hair salon in the break room. Between his four kids, his devoted wife, and a job that kept him running around the country, he was hardly ever at the office. The very fact that he was here today, and not for the purpose of getting his coif done, indicated that strange things were afoot at Century Strategies.

Amanda, Emily, and I grabbed some gray metal folding chairs from the break/beauty salon room and wondered aloud if we might be in trouble. I might have been in trouble, but at the end of the day, I didn't work for Tim, I worked for Ralph. And I knew Ralph well enough to know that he didn't care if I was pole-dancing in my office, or waltzing in at 9:30 A.M. and pretending like I'd been there since 8:30 A.M. as long as my work got done. Which it always did. So I was solid.

We dragged chairs into Tim's office and set them up in a horseshoe around a desk awash with unacknowledged little pink phone message slips.

"Put your tray tables up and get ready for a bumpy ride," said Tim, relishing the drama of the moment. "Ralph is running to become Georgia Republican party chairman."

Our jaws dropped. *Odd,* I thought, *Ralph hasn't mentioned anything to me.*

"I am going to assign each of you counties," Tim continued, unfazed by the looks of bewilderment on our faces. "Within those counties you will need to identify and appoint Reed county leaders."

Georgia has 159 counties, and he divided them up among us. I was anxious to receive my assignment—I was going back on the campaign trail! Except this time, I would be working for a proven winner.

"And Lisa," he said, "you'll have Fulton County and the media, of course." I was crestfallen. Just one district—and Fulton County, of all places? Fulton was home to Georgia's liberal Republicans. In short, it was where all the Ralph-haters resided.

"Can you at least throw me a bone?" I asked Tim. "What about Stephens County?" Ralph was from Stephens County.

"No, Ralph wants you to work Fulton."

Case closed.

We stepped out of Tim's office, energized. Ralph is a forward thinker, so we knew that this signified the beginning of what was to be great things. This was the first step in a much bigger plan. Perhaps he wanted to be Georgia's governor. And then senator. Whatever the ride was, I was aboard. Ralph knew he could win this election easily. He was riding on the wings of the recent Bush election. He knew all the top Republican donors. The timing couldn't have been better for Ralph to reenter politics, this time without the baggage that came with the Christian Coalition.

"Get to work," Tim told us. "You can build faster than you can tear down."

To become chairman of the Georgia Republican Party, each candidate vies to win a majority vote from a preselected group of delegates. Delegates represent all 159 counties and are elected by their peers prior to the statewide Republican convention. The convention is held once every two years. Typically these races are very quiet, inexpensive affairs, off the radar screens of the general public. In fact, just about no one, outside of the party apparatus itself, knows who the chairman of their political parties is, and press coverage for such a lackluster event is rare, if not unheard of. That is, until Ralph Reed entered the race. Once we threw our hat in the ring, the competition blew up. With the amount of press attention he received, one might've assumed Ralph was vying for chairman of the Republican party of the United States of America. We had reporters swooping in from all over the country to interview Ralph, like long-time veteran political reporter Tom Edsall of the *Washington Post*.

"That was weird," Ralph said after I returned from escorting Tom out of the building. "What's the *Post* doing sending a top political reporter down to cover a state chairman's race?" He followed it up with his signature boisterous laugh.

I smiled and shrugged my shoulders. I don't think Ralph minded it one bit.

We had lapel stickers printed and leaflets published featuring Ralph's family and his four-step plan to uniting the party. With this campaign, he was trying to move more toward the middle. The Right Hand of God was twitching, shifting ever so slightly to the center? I was proud of the foresight, strategy, and determination. I was almost in awe.

I was walking past Ralph's office one morning, at the height of the campaign, when he called me in.

"Lisa, what's this with Amanda milking a cow on the radio?"

I tried to remain stoic. I knew exactly what he was talking about.

"Ah. Well. Amanda loves Madonna. You know, the singer?"

"Yes, I'm familiar with Madonna," he said, sighing.

"Okay," I said as I pulled on the ends of my hair (nervous habit) and chattered on. "So, there was this radio contest, and you had to answer a few trivia questions related to Madonna." I continued, "If you answered those right, you advanced to the next level. She had to milk a cow and fill a milk jug faster than the other contestant. It was called 'milking for Moodonna' tickets. Amanda won."

Ralph looked at me, his eyes narrowing ever so slightly.

"Lisa, I've got delegates calling me asking about what my staff is doing on the radio. Please ask her to cut it out. And can you also talk to her about taking down all the Madonna pictures taped to her office walls. It is not appropriate."

I walked over to Amanda's cubby and told her that Ralph requested that she not enter contests with mooing sound effects and lactating farm animals so she could win concert tickets to see the Material Girl. We took down her pictures of a Madonna in torn fishnets, Madonna with yoga muscles, and Madonna in aerobics attire, giggling under our breath.

As the campaign rolled on, Ralph focused on wooing the hard-core workers of the Republican party, or what we in the biz call the "grass-roots." These people are the backbone of any political organization. While some people have the luxury of writing a big check in support of their preferred candidate, these committed constituents give something that's just as valuable: time and energy. These tireless men and women (who often enlist their kids as well) attend the rallies, write the letters to Congress, walk door-to-door passing out campaign propaganda during election years, and stand on the cement islands in the middle of rush hour traffic wearing red, white, and blue hats, waving signs, and chanting campaign slogans. It's hard to beat the church crowd.

Most of them are kind, loving, and down-to-earth people who find peace and meaning in the teachings of Jesus Christ, and comfort in less government involved in their lives. And then there are some who give Jesus a bad name. They organize to vote down the use of medical marijuana and gay marriage and against a woman's right to choose. It troubles me to say this, but I bet the members of the Westboro Baptist Church—

who fly around the country to demonstrate at the funerals of America's fallen soldiers and say things like, "Military funerals have become pagan orgies of idolatrous blasphemy, where they pray to the dunghill gods of Sodom and play Taps to a fallen fool"—vote Republican, too.

The only grassroots worker I encountered who could be classified as "crazy" was a man named Bill. He attended all major Atlanta area sporting events to wave his "Jesus Saves" sign in the air.

"Hey, Bill," I'd say casually, as I strolled into Philips Arena to catch a hockey game.

"Hi, Lisa," he'd answer back with the same casual tone in his voice, like it was perfectly normal to hold a sign calling for salvation in front of a major sporting event. (Despite not being a huge sports fan, I liked to attend games because of the incredible food court at the stadium—sushi, nachos, french fries, and quesadillas, oh my!)

I liked Bill; at least he never tried to convert me. Major league baseball shortstop and third baseman Cal Ripken Jr., unfortunately, can't say the same thing. While attending an Atlanta Braves home game, Bill heard Jesus tell him to save Cal's soul and ran out onto the professional green playing field. Apparently this type of behavior is frowned upon at Turner Field and in his pursuit to save Cal's soul, Bill was wrangled into submission, dragged off the field, and in the scuffle, broke his arm.

I did my best to mine Fulton County for Reed delegates. My sell was straightforward: "He's going to win, so you better get onboard." When I would turn one, which was not easy, they would make me swear not to tell any of their friends or family. Luckily for them, voting was by secret ballot. I volunteered to drive out to the sticks to represent the Reed campaign at local county meetings, attended by the Evangelical crowd, and found myself on first-name terms with true zealots, like Georgia God Squad leader Rebecca Street, a well-preserved, slim, uptight, middle-aged woman who smelled like drugstore perfume and Shower-to-Shower. Her colored hair was hair-sprayed still, and I never saw her without makeup or red lipstick. Her daughter, a lesbian in a committed relationship, ran a Planned Parenthood clinic in San Francisco, which did not go over well with Mama. When Street found out her daughter was gay, she called her "sick," "crazy," and "of the devil." Rebecca, if you are such a loyal banger of the Bible, then you should know the passage from Leviticus: "Thou shalt not lie with mankind, as with womankind." Pretty much a green flag for girl-on-girl action if you ask me. So I say, "Let them eat bush!" Rebecca was a woman I would never have wanted to mingle with, or even have known, had it not been for my work with Ralph. But I learned to coexist with her and all the other Godaphiles. We joined forces, albeit from different angles, for a common goal: to put Republican candidates, my boss included, into office.

And in November of 2003, we succeeded—Ralph was elected chairman of the Georgia Republican Party, with 60 percent of the vote in a three-way race. We lost Fulton, but Tim said we did not lose as horribly as he thought we could have. Ralph gave me a bonus and a raise, and kept me at Century Strategies. Life was good. I was thriving at work, and I had a strong stable of friends whom I loved and trusted. The only thing missing was the thing I hadn't been looking for—a husband. It was around this time that I met Jimmy Baron.

I was at a bar with Amanda and Emily, who spotted Jimmy, a famous rock morning show personality in Atlanta. The girls and I were having a celebratory drink honoring ourselves and all of our hard work on Ralph's successful campaign to become Georgia Republican party chairman. Jimmy was at the bar with his radio station. He was making an appearance, and we were just trying not to make asses out of ourselves (as usual). Jimmy was a funny guy, who added the mischief and smarts to the top-rated morning radio show in Atlanta. Amanda and Emily were both big fans of the show, and as such, they happened to know he was Jewish.

"He's Jewish and you're Jewish!" squealed Amanda. "You should meet!"

She scurried over to Jimmy. "You need to come meet our friend. She's a Jew."

I was so embarrassed. I glanced over at Emily accosting the poor DJ, and my gaze lingered longer than it normally would have. Even though he was wearing an outdated Hawiian print shirt over a faded pair of blue jeans and his hair was cut a little too close to his head, there was something about him I liked very much. I recorded that moment in my head. I knew, in that instant, that this man was going to change my life forever. When Jimmy came over and introduced himself, I was very happy to give him my number.

Jimmy Baron voted Democrat, but at least he didn't whip out his junk on the first date. And he did fall asleep on our second date. That's right, out cold. He asked me to attend a lecture about global peace (or was it global warming—I don't know). We entered the auditorium and took our seats. About fifteen minutes in, I thought I heard some heavy breathing. I was thinking, *Who makes out during a speech on the conflict in the Middle East?* Then I heard a strange whistling noise. I cranked my neck around to see who was sawing logs. I thought once I figured out whose piehole was wide open, I would point them out to Jimmy and together we would share a quiet laugh and create a fond memory. Bad news for me. Jimmy was the phantom snorer.

Ordinarily the second date equals third base for Lisa Gimbel—but we didn't get to third base that night. Jimmy leaned in for a good-night kiss, and I stuck my hand out for a handshake. Hell no! I wasn't putting out. He had fallen asleep on our date! Look, I'm not above looking past a second date misstep. I have had my share of dates who showed up wearing black stone-washed jeans. And it's not out of the question for someone to be asleep at some point in the date. Usually, that point is the next morning. He's asleep and I'm tiptoeing out the door.

But nothing says, I really don't care how this date goes or for that matter I'm really not concerned with impressing you, like falling asleep at the *beginning* of the date. Despite my misgivings, I couldn't shake off the feeling that Jimmy was someone I wanted in my life, so I accepted another date.

Later I would learn that what I thought was an isolated incident of a man being unimpressed with his date, was actually consistent behavior. I guess that's what happens when your day starts at 4:30 am. He would fall asleep everywhere. Speeches, movies, the dinner table—you name it, he's slept there.

Whether he was awake or inappropriately asleep, I soon realized I was in love with Jimmy. Being with Jimmy was helping me grow up. I had bought a bed frame, couch, and corresponding love seat, coffee table, and bookshelf. After the third or fourth date, I offered to make Jimmy dinner. But there was one problem: I didn't have a kitchen table! So, that day, I went to Pier One, bought a bamboo dining room table, had one of my ex-boyfriends go with me to the store and pick up the table, then bring it into my apartment. Dinner went swimmingly, and the next day I returned the table.

Fearful of losing him, I waited to tell Jimmy that I worked for Ralph Reed. This turned out to be a good strategy. Eventually, after around three months of dating, I mustered the courage to tell him who my boss was.

"I'm glad you waited, because, yeah, I would have broken up with you." He laughed. "But I can't now, I'm too far gone."

Jimmy and I had a really sweet love affair that struck the perfect balance between our secular and nonsecular worlds. Jimmy enjoyed my passion for politics and rock music. We went to dozens of concerts, and hung out backstage with rock stars, noting the hangers-on, the gate crashers, and the egos, observing the uncanny similarities between the music world and the political campaign trail.

Friday nights Shabbot dinners belonged to just the two of us, and Saturday nights we could be found anywhere from backstage at a Jane's Addiction concert to wiping off the fake blood that speed metal band GWAR sprayed on us. We shared a passion for travel and anywhere we went, in the world, we always lit the Friday night Shabbat candles and had dinner in our hotel room. I loved the tradition. It made us a couple. A year and a half after we started dating, while we were on vacation in Turks and Caicos, Jimmy proposed. I was in my bathing suit, wading out to collect shells with Jimmy on a small patch of earth in the middle of the Carribbean. I looked up after scooping into my hands a perfectly scalloped shell to find Jimmy on his knees holding a big ol' diamond ring in his hand.

"Lisa, will you marry me?"

"I'm in my bathing suit!" was all I could think of. "Oh, and yes. I will marry you, Jimmy."

I was twenty-eight and he was forty. Eight months later we were married in Phoenix in a big traditional Jewish wedding at the Arizona Biltmore. Ralph was not able to attend—he was too busy.

Our traditional Orthodox wedding was both magical and ethereal. The warm space that held our *chuppah*, the traditional canopy where Jewish couples meet under to marry, was adorned with white roses and forest-green leaves. Two hundred and twenty guests sat theater-style as Jimmy and I were marched down the aisle to the rich voices of personal friends and recording artists Evan and Jaron (of Crazy for the Girl fame). Jimmy came down the white-lined aisle first, stopping right before the chuppah, where we would ascend together to meet the rabbi. I wore a dreamy and elegant strapless Reem Acra crystal-beaded ball gown. My floor-length winter-white veil provided a soft white glow that surrounded my entire being as I floated down the aisle escorted by both of my parents. I stopped to circle my soon-to-be husband seven times. This tradition has several different interpretations; among the reasons, the seven turns around a praying groom represent the seven days of creation and symbolize the new world the couple will create together. Thirty minutes later we were man and wife. Now it was time to get the party started.

Two heavy doors were held open and the sweet smell of hundreds of lush blooming gardenias spilled into the hallways of the five-star hotel.

"Ladies and gentlemen, please help me to welcome, for the first time ever, Mr. and Mrs. Jimmy Baron!" the bandleader exclaimed.

Jimmy and I rushed into the ballroom holding hands and soon let go to begin the the *Hora*! The eight-piece band started playing the fast-paced Israeli music and soon the portioned dance floor, to separate men from women during this custom circle dance (Jews don't line-dance if possible), was packed with partiers. The floor was split by a line of tall, potted topiaries perfectly wrapped in sparkling swatches of exquisite ivory fabric. We were well into the first forty-five minutes of our hour and a half celebratory dance when I noticed that my wedding had party crashers. Two crashers to be specific, and their names were my left boob and my right boob.

With the stress of the lead-up to the wedding, I lost five pounds. This made my dress not quite as fitted as I needed it to be. Lots of sweat and movement softened the boning in the bodice even further. So when I was hoisted up onto my chair to bounce around, something else got bounced out: my tits. Leave it to me to turn my buttoned-up classy religious event into a topless bar. My mother instinctively yanked me off of the chair (remember, this is an Orthodox wedding, and I've got a crew of long-bearded, black-hatted rabbis in attendance) and yelled for my best friend from childhood, Allyson, to do something quick!

They rushed me into the bathroom for a fashion emergency strategy session. One woman, on her way into the stall, suggested hair spray. We looked at the can of Herbal Essence extra hold that sat on the counter, looked back at my ta-tas, and concluded that even industrial-hold, professional-strength hair spray wouldn't hold these jugs into the top of my crumpled (and crumpling) gown.

This singular event may be the one to turn a bride into a bridezilla. But I wasn't willing to let a couple of double Ds stop me from dancing at my wedding. That's why it was I who came up with the master plan.

"Scissors, please," I asked of my team of wedding-day wardrobe consultants (my mom and Allyson).

Allyson (or my mom, I'm not sure which one) ran into the bathroom and removed a pair of tiny manicure scissors we provided to our guests in a self-made vanity kit. (We Gimbels think of everything!)

I pulled off my veil, cut out the comb that attached the six hundred dollars' worth of tulle to my head, and instructed my team to start wrapping. I began to spin around and around until the see-through overpriced accessory was able to contain "the girls." The scene in the bathroom taking place during my wedding looked more like a bachelorette at her bridal party being wrapped in toilet paper in one of those stupid wedding-dress-making contests.

I was back on the dance floor turning out some funky moves, including the robot, in no time. At 1:00 A.M. when my dancing feet could dance no more, I realized that my wedding was magical, beautiful, and semi-pornographic: the perfect way to start a new life!

After I wed, my friends and family hardly recognized the new me. I quit smoking and slowed the party train way down. I turned out to be one of those girls who doesn't have much use for Girl's Night Out when she falls in love—something I didn't know about myself because I had never been in this kind of love before. With Jimmy in my life, suddenly I didn't feel so desperately attached to Ralph anymore.

What I did come to want was a baby.

But instead of a baby, I got a a poorly behaved salt-and-pepper mini schnauzer with an under bite named Jack, despite Jimmy already having two dogs. I got Jack at a charity fund-raiser that I attended with Ralph's wife Jo Anne. I paid $400.00 dollars for this ball of bad and I loved him to the ends of the earth and back. I named him for "Just Jack," from the sitcom *Will and Grace*. I really wanted to name him after my role model Karen (also from the show), but Jack was already exhibiting signs of dys-functional behavior, and I feared that giving him a girl's name would re-ally send him over the edge.

Together we had four dogs. That's right, I said four. Because one day at an outdoor Jewish festival Jimmy and I stumbled upon a dog rescue booth and found Annie. She was skinny, shy and, well, not the prettiest pup in the mix and that's exactly why we bought her. "If we don't take her, no one will." And home she came with us. Annie and Jack became the best of buddies, partners in crime, and playmates until the end.

It was around that time that I heard that South Georgia Congressman Saxby Chambliss was looking for a press secretary in his bid to become United States senator. I was starting to get that nagging campaign itch again, and asked Ralph if he minded loaning me out for a bit. He obliged, saying it would be a smart move for both of us, because Saxby was fa-vored to win his reelection campaign. Saxby was a real laid-back, cool Southern dude who liked to hunt and fish, and I dealt with the media, becoming the voice and face of the campaign until the general election, when I shared the responsibility with another tart. I still talked to Ralph all the time to let him know how things were going. I had no intention of leaving Century Strategies for too long.

After Senator Chambliss was elected, I let myself drift off into domes-tic bliss with Jimmy, working the odd PR job here and there, imagining babies and endless love (cue the Lionel Ritchie/Diana Ross ballad).

And then I got a phone call from Ralph.

"I have a job for you, Lisa Baron," he said.

Chapter 17

Running for Office
with Scissors

The year 2005 was significant for two reasons: I came back to work for Ralph, who now hoped to become the first Republican lieutenant governor of Georgia since Reconstruction and wanted my help in getting him elected. It also came to my attention that I had seen what only a handful of Jewish women have ever seen: a convicted felon's penis. Jason, my blind date arranged by Ralph, was featured in a *Washington Post* story: "3 Charged in Killing of California Man: Businessman Slain after Abramoff Deal."

"You have got to be fucking kidding me," I whispered to myself as I read the headline. My eyes scrolled down as I remembered the details of that night, five years ago, at the Ritz-Carlton. I recalled how Jason had told me about buying something with Jack, but he had never mentioned anything about mobsters, horse heads, fake wire transfers . . . The only thing that had come up in the course of the evening was his weiner.

Jason was not in jail for having anything at all to do with the afore-mentioned murder. He pled guilty to wire fraud, and was seriously impli-cated in the whole Abramoff scandal that would ensue. Thinking about it, I wasn't really all that surprised that Jason was jailed; in fact, I'd bet that a sizeable percentage of guys who charge out of hotel bathrooms waving their junk around like a state carnival pinwheel probably end up behind bars at some point.

But Jack being in trouble was troubling. Jack was one of Ralph's very best friends.

Jack Abramoff was a devout Orthodox Jew. He wore a black hat, fol-lowed a strict kosher diet, and adhered to the laws of the Sabbath. Twenty years ago, he met a young Ralph Reed who had just moved to DC from Georgia, fresh and unjaded. Reed was an intern for the College Republi-can National Committee, of which Jack was the elected chairman. While Ralph found Christ, the other found himself attracted to the discipline and spirituality of Orthodox Judaism. Both found a friend in each other. The bond grew thicker when Ralph introduced Jack to the woman who would become his future wife.

From the CRNC, Ralph was wooed away to help televangelist and former nominee for president of the United States, Pat Robertson. While Robertson's run for president fell short, they amassed something very powerful along the way—the support of hundreds of thousands of voters who all had one thing in common: an unwavering belief in God and the hunger to return the country to one nation under him. Reed helped Robertson create a home for his new army, the infamous, powerful activ-ist machine: the Christian Coalition, a socially conservative, angrier ver-sion of today's Tea Party.

Meanwhile, Jack's career saw him through politics for a few more years until he left to join a prestigious lobbying firm. He began as an assistant, but hard work and smarts, as well as the 1994 Republican take-over of Congress, sent his career into high gear. It helped that his buddy, Ralph, was behind the political tsunami of change that triggered the shift of power in Washington. Some considered the Republican tidal wave just an electoral overcorrection to the left-swerving Clinton years. Either way, it was the perfect storm for Ralph and Jack. Timing is everything, I guess.

Ralph and I made a date to meet to discuss his intention to become Georgia's next lieutenant governor. Ralph was hoping to beat Senator Casey Cagle, the other Republican after the job, and clinch the opportunity to run in the election. Why he couldn't just run for a congressional seat in a safe Republican district before going statewide was beyond me. Especially considering what he was about to tell me. My guess is that he was high off an incredible couple of years as state Republican party chairman. Under Ralph's rule, Georgia elected a Republican U.S. senator, elected the first GOP governor in 130 years, and gained control of the state senate for the first time since Reconstruction. During his tenure, the state party budget increased from $5 million to $10.7 million, the donor base went from 12,000 to 34,000 (remember he put together a massive Rolodex while fund-raising for George W. Bush), and the grass-roots network grew to over 3,000 volunteers. The timing was perfect, he must've thought.

I had an extra spark in my stiletto step on the day I went back to Century Strategies. Of course, Ralph and I had kept in touch via e-mail and the occasional lunch, but after two years, I was excited to be back in these familiar four walls. Yet again, I felt like I had picked a winner. I had started with him from the ground floor, and I was sure I would land a coveted role in whatever administration Ralph Reed found himself the head of. We were political soul mates.

Walking through those two-ton front doors I had the feeling like I was returning home from college. And the band was getting back together! Only we were switching out the lead guitarist (Amanda) and the bassist (Emily), who had moved on since I had left. I bounded down the hall, stopping, briefly, my heart heavy to pay my respects to an empty Cubbyland. While I had been working for the campaign of United States Senator Saxby Chambliss, Amanda had returned to Mississippi to help elect Former Republican National Committee Chairman Haley Barbour, governor. After that, she burnt out and said she was not interested in another campaign. Emily had gotten another job with a member of the Georgia Assembly (our version of Congress).

With or without my girls, at least I still had Big Les. And it felt like this time, I was coming back for good, embarking on a career that was sure to be the envy and inspiration of young politicos like me, who dreamed of a long career with a successful, powerful, and high-profile politician. We'd be known as the wind beneath his/her wings, the real decision-makers, the brains behind the operations. I couldn't believe my luck. I had given my time, paid my dues, and believed in a boss who was now going to be lieutenant governor of Georgia, then governor of Georgia, and then, well, who knows! And I, his trusty aide for so many years, was going with him. Finally, my plan to be the best-dressed number two who ever lived was becoming a reality.

Ralph was the ambitious politician, steadfast in his commitment to morals and values, and I was happy to do all the heavy lifting that needed to be done. Being a leader scared me. It meant picking up the slack that others in the group left undone or not properly done. It meant long hours, little sleep, and all of the blame if something went wrong (bad leadership) or a smidge of the accolades when a project was successful (it's a team effort after all). It's so much easier to be the number-two guy. Think about it. Clinton and Gore, Obama and Biden, George W. Bush and Karl Rove, Paris and Nicole, Bullwinkle and Rocky.

I raced past a couple of new hires, young boys wearing red ties around their neck and idealism on their sleeves, and burst into Big Les's office, my arms open wide as if I was on Broadway. "Did you miss me?"

"Well," she paused, "yes, of course I did!"

Her office looked exactly the same, a desk stacked with papers and personal mementos from friends and Ralph's clients smooshed in between two file cabinets, a computer, and a computer console with a pull-out drawer for the keyboard. "Bush for President" signs were stuck to the walls courtesy of two-sided tape, and pictures of kittens dotted the tops of the cabinets.

My office looked the same, too: industrial, drab, and brown. There was one significant change to it—a new dark-haired girl. Mary Frances Blue. Mary Frances was as scrappy as she was pretty, and as Southern as boiled peanuts and fried chicken. One of four kids, she grew up on Blue Lane on a sprawling plantation in the Georgia country. She has two sisters, both older, and one brother. Fran, as we called her, went to college in Mississippi and upon graduation moved to Washington, DC, to work on Capitol Hill in a political fund-raising firm. After a few years of feast and famine and an urge to get away from politics, Mary Frances went in pursuit of a paycheck, vacation time, and a pension plan. She took a job over at a trade association. Trade associations are where politicos and former congressional aides go to die. Not ready to begin the death march to retirement, she, like I did many years ago, heard that Ralph Reed was looking to hire. It was for a fund-raiser this time. Ralph, being more methodical than any human being I have ever met, brought Mary Frances on board a year before he ever announced his intentions to run for statewide office, so that she could get comfortable and help expand the financial donor list. I had never officially met Mary Frances, but everyone who knew me and knew her always said the same thing: you will love her! And they were right. Even though I think I was the third Jew she ever met in her life, we got on famously.

The door to Ralph's office was closed, but Big Les told me that they were expecting me and just to go on in. With my hair freshly flat-ironed and a little black dress that hit just about at my knees, I pressed the metal handle down on Ralph's door and pushed it open. I felt like Rhoda walking on to the set during a live *Mary Tyler Moore* reunion show.

"Hello!" I said, beaming.

Tim was pacing back and forth like a tiger, and Ralph was sitting behind a desk, a dark expression on his face. He threw a forced smile my way.

"Hey there," Ralph answered. "So, we are raising money and signing up volunteers at twice the speed of any other candidate in history."

I grinned.

"Normally, Lisa," Ralph began, his tone changing, "in a down-the-ballot race like the one I am in, all we would need is a fund-raiser, a fax machine to send out press releases, and maybe some guys with pickup trucks to stick yard signs in the ground around the state, but I've got a situation that I think you need to be made aware of."

"Okay," I responded eagerly.

"Did you ever meet Jack?" he asked.

I nodded yes. He didn't need to specify which Jack for me to know he was talking about Abramoff.

"Well, when I left the Coalition in 1996 to set up Century, Jack was very helpful, he referred a lot of business to me," he said, laying out the facts.

Apparently Jack had left his lobbying firm to join up with the prestigious Washington, DC-based law firm Greenberg-Traurig. Among his clients were Indian tribes who made millions and millions of dollars from slot machines and casinos. A few years back, Ralph had been hired by Jack to implement extensive grassroots campaigns that called for the casinos of rival tribes to be shut down, in the name of God, who does not approve of gambling. By using his reputation to mobilize Christians, Ralph indirectly stopped an initiative to install a statewide lottery system in Alabama (which would have threatened casino earnings), and fought an online gambling bill in Congress. Not because, as the propaganda stated, gambling was an evil thing. But because Jack's clients—other casinos, with a financial interest in shutting down the competition—were paying him. Abramoff funneled the casino moneys to Ralph through other organizations.

When Ralph's made-to-order, anti-gambling rabble-rousing was successful, Jack's casino clients thrived. And Ralph was always successful.

Ralph wasn't the only one playing this game. In fact, there were a lot of other men and women who were tangential figures in the complexity of this vast lobbying scandal, possibly the largest and most widespread in United States history, whose names remain unknown or were quickly forgotten once Abramoff was sentenced. Ralph, on the other hand, was a man who had built his career on religious dogma. His work, while technically not illegal, didn't measure up to his longtime anti-gambling stance. (He had once called gambling a "cancer.") Now he was on the verge of being busted as a Bible-bashing hypocrite, saying he was opposed to the very thing that was making him millions. Five years earlier, while Amanda, Emily, and I were down the hall laughing in the conference room and Big Les was returning e-mails with highlighting foils in her hair, Ralph was crossing the line.

Jack was under investigation. Which was bad enough. But guess who was heading up the United States committee that would be responsible for overseeing the investigation? Remember Senator John McCain? Well, he never did become President of the United States. Ralph took care of that in the 2000 South Carolina primary. What he did become was Chairman of the United States Senate Committee on Native American relations. The same committee that was now investigating Abramoff's gambling operation and Ralph's involvement. Yes, it was five years since the dustup in the South, but McCain was still mad about what went down in the dirty South and everyone knew it . . . including Ralph. Ah, paybacks are a bitch slap.

I can give an educated guess as to what Ralph may have been thinking when he accepted the work from Jack Abramoff. He probably went back and forth in his head as to whether he should do it at all. But the risk of getting caught was small, and the amount of money he would be paid was huge. He needed to amass a considerable fortune to take handsome care of his family while pursuing the nonlucrative path of public life. He told me that he had asked for assurances from Jack that when he did the work, he would not be paid with gambling money. He said he had trusted Jack Abramoff, now one of the most controversial crooks in lobbying history, on his word. And this alone, thought Ralph, would give him the protection he needed (but was never anticipating to need) if ever asked about the work. Like me, Ralph always skated very close to the line, but this time he may have skated too close.

He assured me that the issue of Jack would go away. He could explain it away. After all, he was always the smartest person in the room. I have never been the smartest person in any room, but I already knew that my prophesied career as number two of the untarnished right-lined was now totally fucked, inches away from decimation at the hands of our sworn enemy, John McCain. I felt sick to my stomach.

Ralph had defaulted on his end of our eight-year cooperative effort to take a Christian leader and turn him into a polished politician who represented every constituent. I held up my end of the bargain. I had worked the eighteen-hour days, seven days a week. I had driven all over Georgia at the ass-crack of dawn to lead "Ralph Reed for Republican Party Chairman" grassroots breakfasts. Whatever was asked of me, I did, happily. All Ralph had to do was not do anything immoral or illegal. When Ralph made the decision to work for Jack, who was working for an Indian tribe with gambling interests, he was gambling with my career and everyone else's on his staff, too. We all knew that in politics, that was the risk you took when you aligned yourself so closely with a politician. If they go down, you go down.

Take, for example, South Carolina Governor Mark Sanford. Sanford, fast on his way to Republican party stardom, was sandbagged. Hailing from the important presidential primary state of South Carolina, a congenial and physically attractive conservative governor, he was the head of the Republican Governor's Association, and rumors had him pegged as a sure thing for a vice presidential pick in an upcoming presidential election. That is until his penis led him down to South America. Talk about thinking with the wrong head. This normally levelheaded, astute governor let his third leg do the talking and quite literally, the walking. No, he wasn't hiking his beloved Appalachian mountain trail as he claimed. He was following the happy trail all the way down to Venezuela, where he claimed his soul mate lived. Which was a problem, because his wife lived in South Carolina. When he made the decision to stray, he not only threw away his career, he took down the dreams and ambitions of his longtime political team that had been loyal and determined for so many years. Their dreams of moving East went limp when Sanford went south. And then there is the tale of the congressman who just wanted a little tail—male tail, that is: Florida Congressman Mark Foley who got caught "sexting" (a text message filled with sexy content) to underage male congressional pages. That kind of behavior goes over great in Republican circles. While Ralph has always been a gentleman and true to his wife (which is rare these days), he wasn't righteous in his professional choices. For those who counted on him for a career, he was unfaithful.

In the spirit of full(ish) disclosure, now felt like as good a time as ever to mention my new side project. Shortly before rejoining Century Strategies, I had taken on a side job as a columnist at an Atlanta start-up weekly called the *Sunday Paper*. It was a hip, artsy publication and my first person-style editorial, called "Committed," was about the trials and tribulations of my life as a wife, wannabe mom, and woman in the world. I loved it because it presented me with the first opportunity I'd ever had to express my own thoughts and opinions (rather than someone else's) and because it allowed me to showcase the talent I had developed with Ralph—my writing.

"Of course I'll quit if you want me to," I said, holding my breath and crossing my fingers.

"Keep your writing, it shouldn't be a problem," he said. "This should go away for us by December."

I exhaled. A little of my anger dissipated. I was glad Ralph hadn't laid down the law. And maybe he was right; maybe there was some way this Abramoff business could be neatly swept away under the carpet.

The next day we were off to Washington, DC, to meet with Ralph's team of white-collar crime attorneys. While we were there, one of our three opponents for lieutenant governor dropped out of the race. Things, believe it or not, actually looked great for the Reed campaign. We had raised more money than any Republican nominee in the state of

Georgia—for either party. We had more yard signs in more yards, we had thousands of volunteers, and our Reed for Lieutenant Governor phone banks were being manned by hoards of supporters. Reed was considered a sure thing, a shoe-in, the heir apparent. But the voters, and I think even we, didn't feel the vibrations of the tsunami that was about to hit.

Chapter 18

"Ralph Loves Jews"

Ralph's campaign office was leased in the same building as Century Strategies, one floor above the corporate office. Our accommodations were identified by a flimsy sheet of white copy paper, stuck to the right door frame with a single piece of clear Scotch tape, reading "Ralph Reed for Lt. Governor." There were three main offices, a conference room in the middle, and off to the left, a wide-open space that was buzzing with volunteers. I, the communications director, took an office; Mary Frances, the finance director, got another; and Jared, our newly hired twentysomething redheaded political wonder-boy, fresh off of a congressional win in an important Republican district, occupied the corner office with the view. Yes, it was a view of the parking lot, but it still provided a window out onto a world that would soon be turning its eyes upon us.

We started the campaign with a political director, but after three months he quit. Amanda wouldn't join the campaign because she was burned out, and Emily was working with her state senator at that time. Big Les remained Ralph's assistant and office air traffic controller, and she remained one floor below us outside of Ralph's sanctum.

The first thing that greeted visitors upon entry into the Ralph Reed for Lieutenant Governor headquarters was Intern Jeff, a friendly, chubby kid with a head filled with sandy-brown curls and a neck full of handmade hippie beaded necklaces. Of course, he wasn't a real hippie—in fact, he hailed from a prominent and wealthy Republican family. And judging from Jeff's Haight-Ashbury-inspired work ethic, I suspect his daddy donated the maximum amount possible to Ralph's campaign. I couldn't imagine how else he had ended up at our front desk—internships are like gold for anyone with political aspirations. Many of today's most successful political stars and television talking heads began their careers fetching coffee, answering phones, and entering voter information into a database. Because campaigns run on donations, most of which need to be used to buy television commercials and the time on each television station to run them, they are often run by a skeleton crew, which means that extra hands are always needed and welcomed. So while you may start by asking the campaign manager if he wants you to save room for cream and sugar, you might end up asking the candidate if he was happy with the speech you wrote for his talk at the Rotary Club.

Intern Jeff, on the other hand, wasn't particularly interested in any of that. The kid, in his early twenties, was sick at least six times a month, and his absences, sometimes for three days at a time, suspiciously tended to coincide with when Widespread Panic was in town for a concert. Not a fan of the jam band myself, Mary Frances was the one who astutely made this call. Intern Jeff was responsible for a few memorable office decorations, like the following editorial delight: a page torn from *People* magazine featuring fallen *Full House* star Jodie Sweetin. Intern Jeff had blacked out one of her teeth and attached a dialogue bubble to her mouth that read: "I'm a meth whore." Despite his continuous battle with the cocktail flu, I liked Intern Jeff, even though I don't really know what he did all day aside from read *People* magazine and twiddle his beads.

My office was utilitarian. I had a desk, a computer, a window, and a gynormous dry-erase board, on which I scrawled the names of those unfortunates who were "on notice" or "dead to me." A bright red horizontal line of demarcation separated the "on notice" folk from the "dead to me's." The idea was a complete ripoff from *The Colbert Report*. Every few weeks, Stephen Colbert would call into question politicians, celebrities or ideas and place them into the two aforementioned categories. And likewise, at the end of every day, the entire Reed for Governor staff would gather in my office to air their grievances.

This exercise in bogus power was rather cathartic. There was something very powerful about picking up a black dry-erase marker, pulling off the cap, releasing its formaldehyde-ish smell and smearing the name of a person, persons or object transversely on an over-sized office supply.

So far, in the "on notice" column, were: the copy machine, Big Les for telling Ralph that Mary Frances didn't get into the office until after 1:00 P.M. instead of the pre-rehearsed "she's in the bathroom, I'll have her call you when she gets back to her desk"; the camel toe of Christian front lady Rebecca Street (discovered by Mary Frances at a fund-raiser); Raj, the late-night desk clerk at Kinko's who said it would be "no problem" to have 500 campaign fliers printed by 8:00 A.M. but didn't have them until noon; and Chairman of the United States Senate Commission on Indian Affairs Senator John McCain. In the "dead to me" column were our opponent for lieutenant governor, and a UPS driver who had run over Schnauzer Jack.

With news of the emerging Abramoff scandal relatively under wraps, our campaign was still full steam ahead. Our first big campaign event was the Friday before Father's Day, a "Faith, Family, and Freedom" rally in a conference center located in the Republican-rich county of Cobb. This was to be a huge event, with hundreds of supporters, and thousands of dollars pouring in for the VIP reception. This was our time to shine, dominate, and show Georgia we came to play. The event featured perennially popular and beloved former Democratic United States senator and governor, Zell Miller, and über-famous conservative radio rock star Sean Hannity, who is from Georgia.

In the run-up, the entire campaign staff, regardless of rank, would spend Sunday mornings sprinting around church parking lots, inserting Christian Coalition pro-family scorecards under windshield wipers. With each snap of a wiper, I became more and more resentful that I wasn't back at my apartment, on the couch in my old man pajamas, tending to my hangover by eating french fries, drinking a sixteen-ounce 7-Eleven Coca-Cola, and watching the Sunday morning political talk shows. I hated doing it. I always walked away with the feeling that I just egged someone's house. But literature dropping, or "lit-drops," as we refer to them in the business, was a hell of a lot better than getting assigned to yard sign duty, which included the huge four-by-four that was prominently and strategically placed on the busiest of intersections. And if the opposing campaign got a better yard sign position then you did, you had some serious explaining to do. This often resulted in the mysterious disappearance of the rival's campaign signs.

The day before the big rally, I sat in my office perusing work-related e-mails, making media passes for the members of the Fourth Estate who had indicated they would be in attendance. While I worked, I could hear the homeschoolers, our most loyal block of volunteers, contact voters to come to the rally. "Hello, this is Tripp. I'm calling on behalf of the Ralph Reed for Lieutenant Governor campaign to let you know about the Reed for Lieutenant Governor Rally. Oh yes, he will fight for our values. He most definitely supports the right to bear arms, it says so right there in the United States Constitution." I could hear the scratch of pubescent voices as they maneuvered through the questions, talking from a pre-approved sheet that listed all of Ralph's stances on issues important to Republican primary voters.

"Well, ma'am, he believes that it's illegal. And that's nothing against illegal immigrants—Mr. Reed is the grandson of Irish immigrants. Oh no, ma'am, he does not support the right for gays to be married. Marriage is a sacred union between a man and a woman."

"Oh yes, ma'am, it's terrible what those liberals say about Mr. Reed, they just don't have any ideas of their own, so they launch personal, negative attacks," he continued. "Oh yes, ma'am, I'm sure it will backfire."

Who knows if the lady on the other end of the line ever showed up to the rally—our main hope was that she would show up when it counted, on Election Day. (But only if she was going to vote for Ralph, otherwise I hoped she stayed home.) I took a break from my desk and wandered into the open area where some young volunteers were decorating white poster boards for use at the rally. I had some creative differences with some of the poster artists. With Ralph standing a relatively petite five-eight in his ostrich boots, I put the kibosh on "Stand Tall for Reed." I also ix-nayed "Ralph Loves Jews." While it may be true that he does indeed love Jews (Evangelicals do believe that Jewish people are indeed God's chosen ones), I suggested something more appropriate.

"That looks great," I said to the doe-eyed girl wearing long sleeves and a long skirt, "but what would you think, maybe, if we said something like, 'Ralph stands with Israel'?"

After completing the day's deposits, Mary Frances came out of her office to see what she could get the volunteers for lunch. They wanted pizza, no cheese. "It hurts our tummies," they told Mary Frances. They asked for soda, no caffeine. The next day was Friday, the day of the big rally, and everyone needed their rest.

CHAPTER 19

Game On

This steamy Southern day—fast on its way to becoming a pit-staining June night—wasn't just another glad-handing, baby-passing, autograph-signing, lapel-sticker-wearing, meet-and-greet kind of day. Today was the much-anticipated, heavily hyped Ralph Reed for Lieutenant Governor Rally! The Cobb Galleria, the site of the event, was already buzzing with excitement when I arrived. Some would argue that with the end of the Clinton administration came the end of the middle ground in politics. Today, there is right and wrong—people voted in absolutes, and with divisiveness comes passion. And these people, primary voters, had passion.

"Hi, Lisa, sweetheart," one of our most ardent supporters said, greeting me with a warm hug. "I saw your name in the newspapers, again, your parents must be so proud!"

"Oh yes. They're just beaming. Sort of," I said, flatly and hugging her back.

Jared and I had arrived early to ensure everything would go smoothly. I needed to be there to troubleshoot any press issues that might arise, such as non-functioning microphones, and Internet access for the print reporters so they could file their stories. And I was excited to meet the journalists with whom I would be working so closely over the course of the campaign. Jared handled everything else, including supporters who thought they should meet Sean Hannity, and one who carried a pocket-sized United States Constitution with him at all times and wanted his book signed. There were a handful of others who heard rumors that Ralph's name had come up in reference to the Jack Abramoff scandal. Were these rumors true? they asked. Jared assured them there was nothing to worry about.

After conducting my sound check on the mult box, and a white paper check, I stepped carefully off of the stage and pointed my round-toe heels directly toward the epicenter of my reality: the press. A row of laptop computers glowed with green lights backlighting the long faces of the print media, a group that I christened the League of Doom. The League was the gaggle of Atlanta press that followed and reported on our campaign. In the line was a twenty-two-year-old recent college grad, assigned to the campaign by the Associated Press. I recognized a rotund political blogger in his late sixties with chronic back pain and a well-known addiction to muscle relaxers. I noticed a gap in their ranks and breathed a sigh of relief—their ringleader, John Haman, wasn't there.

Haman was the leader of the pack, not because of his cunning reporting skills or super investigative powers, but because he was the reporter from the state's largest newspaper, and some might argue, the only newspaper of record in the entire state of Georgia: the *Atlanta Journal Con-*

stitution. A stout man, Haman had a giant-sized head with scant hair. His breath was always labored. Around his neck he wore his company-issued press ID, and his pocket, at all times, contained a mini-tape recorder and a small pad of sweat-furled paper. He kind of reminded me of Mr. Potato Head. He believed that political press tarts, like me, existed to perform two tasks: lie or spin, and not much else. A political sycophant who specialized in getting it wrong, he was cynical, addicted to fast food, and would become the first (and last) journalist I ever raised my voice to.

I held my packet of press releases tight against my body and proceeded toward the anxious pack of press like a zookeeper at feeding time. There were reporters, producers and cameras, and bloggers, everywhere. The TV producers immediately began begging me for time to talk with Ralph, which you always want to honor, because more people watch TV than read the newspaper. What's ironic about this setup, is that TV is dependent on the newspapers for content. Newspapers drive the content because they usually have more dedicated investigative reporters on staff than a station. So what the newspaper reports, television reports, with television producers often accepting what is printed as fact. This is why newspaper reporters carry more weight . . . usually literally. I went down the row of laptops, introducing myself to those I hadn't met yet, shaking hands with the national reporters who had flown in to document Ralph's first political race, and handing my business card to anyone who would take it.

Constituents began to fill the ballroom. Volumes of "Reed for Lt. Governor" stickers were handed out at the door by a squad of volunteers. NRA supporters wore buttons emblazoned with "You can pry my gun from my cold dead hands" while the pro-lifers brought signs that celebrated babies and one girl had a button that read, "I regret my abortion."

At the final count, over a thousand raucous rallies filled the hall, and Mary Frances texted to say that we had just raised over $300,000. I looked down at my watch and noticed that we had five minutes to go until showtime. Jared sent me a text to let me know that Ralph, Zell Miller, and Sean Hannity were on their way in, so I let the media know to get ready. The lights went down, and the patriotic music went up.

The moment the three men entered the stage, cameras were removed from their tripods, print reporters leapt out from behind their desks, and radio announcers grabbed their microphones. I slipped in and out of the throng like a thread of yarn being looped through a cross stitch. I tucked myself near the front of the stage, in between where my boss stood and the press lay waiting.

Campaign rallies are exciting, even for me, and especially those where Ralph is speaking. The boom of his voice and the conviction in his words made people believe that if we just worked together and did exactly what he said, the world could be changed. And not in a generation or two—change was possible now.

"Thank you all very much," he said, waving and drinking in the fever of the event. "Please join me in welcoming my wife, who will be a fabulous Second Lady for the state of Georgia!"

The crowd erupted in applause again. Ralph launched into his stump speech.

"There are some who claim that those values—and the candidates who espouse them—are a liability at the ballot box. Don't you believe them."

The crowd went wild. They roared and clapped, whooped and hollered. The moment was intoxicating.

"The values that you and I cherish . . . are not an albatross—they are the key to our majority." He paused, reached under the dais, and took a swig of bottled water. "From those beliefs we must not flag, we must not fail, we must not retreat." And this is when he unveiled the New Millennium Ralph Reed: "I am a mainstream, balanced budget, tax-cutting, pro-family candidate!"

Pandemonium broke out. Homemade signs bobbed in the sea of people like buoys in a trans-Atlantic storm. Even I was caught up in the fervor, and I am completely used to this shit. The speech, powerful and provoking, was a canvas of carefully chosen words and policy that sought to move him from his right-wing corner box to the middle of the political landscape. But his bread and butter, the red meat he threw to the crowd of hungry voters, was the sprinkling of conservative hyperbole that had been responsible for his meteoric rise from intern (yes, he was actually Zell Miller's intern) to political star.

Like every politician these days, his diatribe ended by thanking the Almighty.

"Thank you, God bless you, and God bless the great state of Georgia."

The thunder of hands clapping roused my attention once again, because this time Ralph was beginning his descent into the crowd, working the rope line first. Mothers were handing him their babies, and he kissed and returned each one. Pictures were snapped, hands were being shaken, "thanks" were distributed, and promises made. "I won't forget who put me there," Ralph told a middle-aged man while they shook hands.

"Ralph," I yelled, "we need to continue to walk back toward the cameras."

"Okay," he acknowledged with a nod.

The camera loved Ralph. We went down the row of tripods, giving good sound bites to each and every one. When the TV interviews ended,

Ralph and I walked to the far corner of the packed ballroom to conduct a mini-press conference with the League of Doom.

"Ralph, first of all, congratulations, this was a great event," said AP boy. "What do you see as the big obstacles ahead?"

"Well, thank you, I think today was a great day, but we have a long, hard fight ahead of us and I'm going to run a race like I am seven points behind."

"Ralph," said another, sticking his tape recorder up to my candidate's mouth, "as the former head of the Christian Coalition, and a man who has never held public office, do you think you are a lightning rod? Do you think the Dems are licking their chops at the thought of running against you?"

Ralph answered, "Like I said in my speech, I'm a mainstream, broad-gauged leader who will seek to serve all of Georgia's citizens. I'm an inclusive leader who holds to principles in his governing philosophy but seeks to build bridges and bring others to the table."

Not satisfied with the answer, the reporter continued, "It just seems odd that you would want to be lieutenant governor, a position that has virtually no power. Is this a stepping-stone to governor?"

"I'm focused on the task at hand," Ralph said without missing a beat. "You know, I live by the motto that Vince Dooley had as head football coach at Georgia: I'm playing Saturday's game."

As my reporter went in for a third helping of Ralph, I shut the impromptu press conference down. "Okay, guys, thank you so much for coming, we will see you all very, very soon. If you need anything, more information, whatever, just call or e-mail me. You have my card."

"That was a great event, huh?" asked Ralph as we walked down the hall away from the noise.

"It sure was," I said.

"What are the chances the media reports it as such?" he wondered aloud.

"Slim to none," I answered, and we both shook our heads and smiled on the truth.

Today was indeed a good day. But while we had excited our base of voters, we had ignited our enemies into action.

CHAPTER 20

Meet the Press

I hope that you have, by this point, gotten to know me fairly well. I am a lot like you (please don't take this as an insult), in that I maintain a pretty good balance between work and play, and I definitely enjoy the play more than the work. I'm neither a right-wing hard-liner nor a liberal tree hugger—I hover somewhere in the middle, with a lean more toward the right. I don't have an ax to grind (except apparently against Ari Fleischer, bow ties, and the District of Columbia), and I hold pretty much everyone in the same measure of contempt, except for my friends and family. But you need to know, and I am here to tell you, that the media suck. (I make an exception for my beloved John Harwood and ABC News's Jake Tapper on account of their hotness.) Almost without exception, most of the news coverage you consume each day will somehow be slanted, distorted, tangled, fudged, or muddled. It has been my experience that print is far more fallible than broadcast. Perhaps it is because they feel obliged to be pessimistic and suspicious in order to do their jobs properly, and ask the kind of questions that unearth stories. This fact, combined with a crumbling print media climate, was more bad news for our campaign.

The *AJC*, like the rest of the country's newspapers, was struggling to stay afloat. In recent weeks, the managing editor had ordered a significant reorganization, and through a memo, which was made public, she announced that circulation would soon drop off in ten counties surrounding the Atlanta metropolitan area. She promised to grow digitally, create more regular enterprises that readers could not get elsewhere. She vowed to improve news and information gathering—and then she cut a dozen departments and offered buyout plans for those employees over fifty. With an industry desperate to survive at any cost, the already dysfunctional relationship between the politicians and the media wasn't going to get better anytime soon. By running for public office at such a dire time, Ralph was opening himself up to attack, I could feel it.

"Ralph doesn't know how to lose, he can only win," Big Les reassured me while I picked the orange M&M's out of her candy dish. I guess she could tell I was worried. Maybe she was right. He was after all, Ralph Reed, the wonder boy of the religious right. I kept reminding myself of that.

College, while very efficient in instructing up-and-comers on how to manage a budget and come up with a winning campaign slogan, does not offer classes on what to do if your candidate is caught with his love wand in a young man's mouth, has a penchant for stealing money from campaign coffers, or dabbles a little bit in some late-night tickle and grab. That's why I homeschooled myself from the ultimate political textbook— Howard Kurtz's *Spin Cycle*. Kurtz, using former White House Press Secretary Mike McCurry as a constant example, teaches you that your job as press secretary/communications director is twofold: protect your boss, and defend what you know to be the truth. To that end, you don't ever want to know too much about anything that could potentially force you to lie to the media. Once a spokesperson loses credibility, they lose their ability to effectively to do their job. That's why I knew, when it came to the Jack Abramoff stuff, I had to strike a balance between being culpable and capable.

The problem for me was twofold: to effectively manage a crisis in the midst of a legal drama, less is more. It's one thing to have a public-relations problem; it's a whole other thing to have a legal one. In the midst of an election, more is more. Voters want and deserve transparency. But when you have a legal issue, less is best. Why? Because you don't want to create a problem through interviews or statements that didn't already exist or contradict your earlier story.

The afterglow following the full release of our mind-blowing rally officially ended when Pulitzer Prize–winning journalist Sue Schmidt from the *Washington Post* (WP) called my cell phone. The *Post* was leading the coverage on the Jack Abramoff scandal, and would publish the saga in installments. The call didn't stick in my brain because of the way she tried to intimidate me, or became verklempt at the idea that I wasn't into pulling my car over on I-85 South during rush hour so that I could answer her questions. It was because she sounded exactly the way you would expect Marge Simpson's sister, Selma Bouvier, to sound if she were a working journalist calling you on your way home from work at 6:30 on a Friday afternoon. Kind of like an angry eighty-year-old woman who wasn't afraid to chase a cigarette with some whiskey while trying to intimidate you with questions she already knows the answer to. Unlike our friend Haman, she never ever got a fact wrong. Which is probably why she won the 2006 Pulitzer Prize for her investigative reporting of the Abramoff affair.

It makes sense that a paper such as the *Post*, based in DC, would be most likely to have the best contacts who would provide them with the juiciest information. Our hometown paper, the *AJC*, not so much. That's why they set about playing a clumsy but ceaseless game of catch-up. Every time the *Washington Post* wrote a story, another story would pop up in another national rag, and then the *AJC* would write a story about the story about the story. *Why*, I wondered, *do the people of Planet Earth need three stories written about the same thing?*

Because they smelled blood, that's why. Moderates in the Republican party were just starting to become comfortable with the idea that Ralph wasn't evil and wearing religion as a cover-up—if they could continually link him to the scandal, the *AJC* knew it would sell a lot of papers.

I got a call from Haman that he was doing a rewrite of a story that had appeared in another national (now defunct) newspaper, the *Boston Globe*.

"Lisa," said Haman, "I've got just a few questions as a follow-up to the *Globe* story, which I am assuming you saw?"

"Yes, I did. Are we on the record, or are you just asking me for background now as you gather your information?" I asked, knowing that when talking to the media you are never really off the record.

"Background is fine," he answered, "we don't need to go on the record yet."

I had just pulled into the driveway, I wanted to finish the call before getting out of the car, and I was concerned about losing reception.

"John," I said, "as we go through this, if you have any questions or concerns or you need me to clear something up, please just ask me. It's in all of our best interests to get the correct information. I am happy to do so. Again, all you have to do is ask."

The questions spanned from "how well did Ralph know Jack?" to "let's talk about stopping the proposed state-sponsored lottery in Alabama" and "do you know who Jack's clients are?" Haman wanted to know how much Ralph really knew about what was happening behind the scenes. After all, he and Jack were very, very close, weren't they?

I took the questions, and told Haman I would get his answers and call him back by the end of the day. As I hung up the phone with Haman, I knew for sure that we wouldn't have the luxury of just one opponent in this race—now we also had the media. It was like having to fight with your boyfriend and his mother.

I called Ralph to see where he was and he told me to come down to the eighth floor to go over the questions. As I mentioned, I had learned that to effectively manage a PR crisis in the midst of a legal drama, less is more. But we are in the middle of a primary campaign, so more is more.

There was no way we could or should ignore what was happening. But at this point in the campaign, my hope was that we would answer the questions in total, do this two or three times, scratch the local media's itch to play keep-up, and then move on to issues that actually mattered to voters. Oh, was I wrong.

I went downstairs and walked briskly toward Ralph's office. At her desk, Big Les had her face mashed up to the computer screen.

"I can't find my damn glasses," she said, sensing my presence in the room. "You here to see Ralph?" she asked.

"Yes, although I wish I wasn't," I said.

"What do you mean? You are in love with Ralph Reed, when do you ever not want to see him?"

"When I have a fist full of media questions that have to do with Jack Abramoff," I said, somberly.

Big Les paused.

"It's bad, isn't it?" she said, flopping back in her chair.

"We are about to find out."

"Hey," I said to Ralph as I walked into his office.

"Hey," he said in a low voice, minimizing his computer screen.

I opened my notebook and turned to my list of questions. I was nervous. Even though these weren't my questions, it felt like I was doing the interrogating. And frankly, part of me felt like I didn't want to know all the answers—if I knew the full truth, it might put me in a position where I had to lie to the media. Spinning is fine, yes. Tell the story in a way that puts my candidate in a positive light, of course. Lie, no.

I cleared my throat and launched in.

The first question was in regard to a Century Strategies' grassroots campaign that stopped a state-sponsored lottery system. Lotteries are considered competition for casino gaming.

"Question number one: The Christian Coalition was very vocal against stopping the proposed state sponsored lottery. Was your firm behind their involvement?"

I paused, swallowed, and looked up at Ralph weakly.

"Yes, we worked with the Coalition of Louisiana. They, like myself, have a long-standing grudge against legalized gambling—which is what the lottery is," he said.

"Question number two: Did you know that an $850,000 donation from Americans for Tax Reform to the Christian Coalition had its origins with Indian casinos?"

It looks iffy when an Indian tribe with gambling interests makes a donation to a politically conservative group. Why? Because social conservatives are traditionally anti-gambling. Why? Because gambling tends to attract drunks, whores, and addicts, folks who aren't traditionally associated with family values, some of whom I call friends.

Ralph's answer: "He's coming after Grover, too? Why would he pick a fight with a guy who, with a single computer keystroke, can e-mail million of Republican donors?"

When Ralph said "he," he was not referring to John Haman, the reporter. The "he" he was referencing was United States Senator and Chairman of the United States Committee on Native American Affairs John McCain. Ralph knew that the information being released to the media, including what would be hundreds of leaked e-mails, was information that only the committee had access to.

Grover Norquist is the executive director of the powerful Americans for Tax Reform. Norquist grew up politically alongside Ralph. They both cut their teeth campaigning on behalf of Reagan, heading up their alma maters' college Republican chapters. While other boys their age were getting laid and high, Ralph and Grover were dropping pro-gun leaflets and Ralph was getting arrested at anti-abortion rallies. In the end, Grover's loins burned with the passion to kill taxes, and Reed went in hot pursuit of protecting society's first set of laws—the Ten Commandments.

Ralph's answer: "Americans for Tax Reform is a nonprofit, they don't have to disclose who their donors are. Haman is fishing, and since he doesn't know, we don't have to answer that question—just refer him to Grover."

The next question, number three, addressed what became known as the use of "shell operations" to obscure the origins of the funding. Shell operations, actually quite common in the grassroots campaigning business, are organizations set up by third parties to appear as if they are nonpartisan. Why? It looks better and oftentimes they are the sort of organizations that can get around paying taxes.

"Question number three: Did you know the $300,000 donation to Citizens Against Legalized Lottery had the same origins?"

Ralph's answer: "That's a trick question," he protested calmly. "That question implies that the money originated with casinos, and the money did not come from casinos, that I know for sure. Correct him on the way that question was asked and tell him—off the record—that you know for certain no casino money was used."

I hesitated. "Tell him that you know for certain no casino money was used." My mind raced. *Do I really know for certain? Is Ralph just telling me what I want to hear, too?* I shuddered and banished such thoughts from my head.

The next few questions dealt with how much money pundits were speculating Ralph had made on the work. I think they all were just trying to figure out how rich Ralph Reed really was.

Question number four: The monies described above, totaling $1.5 million, as documented by the Louisiana secretary of state, indicate that Century Strategies received $1.1 million of the $1.8 raised to defeat the lottery. What was your cut?"

Ralph's answer: "Be very clear on this, Lisa. We did not pocket that money. I didn't get $1.5 million in cash. We paid that money to direct, produce, and place television ads, and we did some direct mail, too."

"How much did the firm take in?" I asked as a follow-up, assuming that's the follow-up I will get with a stonewall answer like that.

"Just answer, 'The industry standard,' but we are not going to get into this business of answering question after question about something that has nothing to do with this campaign."

One dealt directly with Abramoff and Reed's friendship. I looked gingerly up at Ralph. "Do you feel you were duped by Jack?"

Ralph answered, this time sternly and with warning in his voice, "No. Under no circumstances are you to say that I was duped by Jack, let's be very clear about that."

His visceral reaction said to me that Ralph was concerned about what Jack would think of him. Worried that Jack was sitting down in a government office somewhere with a cup of water, being questioned behind a two-way mirror while having press coverage read to him, with quote after quote from associate after associate pleading their innocence, blaming it all on Jack. Like Congressman Bob Ney, who tried to act all innocent and said that he had no idea who super-lobbyist Jack Abramoff even was. He's now former Congressman Bob Ney, and he went to jail to serve a thirty-month prison term for corrupt dealings with now-convicted lobbyist Jack Abramoff.

"Anything else?" he asked setting his bottled water down on top of a coaster.

"Haman says he's got some e-mails that confirm that you knew that the money originated with Indian tribes, so I'm guessing he's probably going to press me on that a bit in his follow-up questions. Do you know what e-mails he is talking about?"

"Lisa, I am being asked about e-mails and work I did six years ago, so without seeing the e-mails, I don't recall. But I'll be damned if I'm going to let that closet Democrat—he hates our party, you know—get in here and try to divert our campaign and take us off message. I'm going to draft a statement that I want you to look at, and then, after today, we are going to give to the media anytime they call."

"Gotcha," I said. I could tell this was going to be a long campaign.

"So," I said, filling the silence, "I'll call Haman back, give him our answers, and then wait for your statement." I fixed my skirt so as not to give a shot of my Spanx while standing up.

"By the way," he said, getting up to stretch, "get Jared to find some-one to drive me to the airport. We probably should start looking for a full-time driver. We need to ramp up a bit here."

CHAPTER 21

Call Off the Dogma

I f you're a girl, imagine you're a guy. If you're a guy, you can still be a guy, but now you're a guy in jail. Now everybody, imagine that you have been cornered by a bunch of really angry felons who have been locked up for years, with no hope of ever getting out. These felons, the angry ones with no hope, but unusually high levels of testosterone, want to make you their bitch. So they bend you over, sans Astroglide. This is what reading the newspaper article that Haman ran felt like.

The two things that would really hurt us would be Ralph being accused of taking gambling money, and Ralph suggesting that he was tricked by Abramoff. The headline over the front-page newspaper article screamed (and I screamed when I read it): "Casino Cash Fed Ralph Reed's Alabama Fight." The jump (a term that refers to the continuation of the story on a different page) read: "Gamblers Fuel Reed's Fight."

We were so fucked, sans lube, bent over the sink, doggy-style.

And then I came upon this unfortunate stanza: "Reed spokesman Lisa Baron said this week that Reed was unaware of the source of the money. Any blame, she said, rests with Abramoff, the Washington lobbyist."

"A sphincter says what!!!!!!!" I said to myself, but loud enough that even the neighbors could hear. I have said a lot of ridiculous things in my life, like the time I told my brother not to put the horse before the cart, or when I told my sister that she had won the war but not the battle, or when I asked my husband if I could buy a $400 pair of shoes. But I had been a press tart long enough to know better than to say anything that I was explicitly asked not to say. Particularly in the legal environment in which we were working.

"RR CELL" appeared in the window of my BlackBerry.

"This is Lisa."

"Hey," said the low, steady, throaty voice on the other end of the line.

The impregnable silence game. I had approximately three seconds to start spinning the story to him in a more positive light, thereby making him feel better about taking a two-by-four to the head.

"Can you believe it?" he said.

"No, I cannot," I said, because I could not.

"What are we going to do? These guys out-and-out lied. They have no proof whatsoever that the money I was paid to do a job, that I did and did well, came from gambling."

"I know, and I was very clear to tell him, off the record, like you instructed, that we know that the money did not come from gambling," I said.

"What are we going to do?" he repeated. "You gotta call Haman's editor and let him know that this is garbage."

"And he wrote," I snuck in while Ralph was still mad at the reporter, "that I said that you said we blamed Jack, and I specifically said we do not blame Jack, because you said specifically that you do not blame Jack."

"Unbelievable," Ralph repeated. "Well, did you say that?"

"No, of course not!" I said. "I said what we talked about. And not only that, after he and I talked for hours, I sent him over our statement."

"You gotta call his editor. We are owed a retraction," Ralph said.

This was like the Microsoft debacle from 2000—only now it was 2005, and I didn't know if I could pull off something like this, not with the stakes this high, not in the middle of a campaign, and not with a newspaper that so hated Ralph. But you never know until you try. Plus, I had a bitch to cut and his name was Haman.

I called him, and did what I had never done, and have never done since—I yelled at a reporter. "Do you have an ax to grind?" I fumed.

I knew he was more interested in earning accolades at his job than getting the story correct. And he knew it, too. He was reveling in the decline of Ralph. I had nothing to lose by yelling at Haman—he was on a smear campaign.

Then I called his editor, who was as appalled as we were. He apologized immediately and offered, drumroll please: *a retraction!* I understood how David must've felt, standing there, shaking, unsure he had truly knocked out Goliath. Holy shit—I did it!

"We got them," I told Ralph, and I could hear him smiling through the phone.

I felt vindicated; I had taken on Haman and his poor journalism, and won. The sense of victory was brief—one hour later, an e-mail from the editor appeared in my inbox. It said that he needed to correct what he said to me earlier. The *AJC* was retracting its offer of a retraction. They would not even correct the headline. Instead, they were going to take an even closer look at the issues Ralph and I raised, and would get back with me later. He then apologized for prematurely offering us a retraction.

Now we were really fucked. No lube, bent over the sink, ball-gagged kind of fucked. We took a big ol' swipe at the king, but we didn't kill him. We just made him mad. I was devastated. It was not in the cards for me to become the Donna Brazile to their Bob Woodward. So now there would not only be no retraction, we were getting another front-page story that would take a look at whether or not the headline was true. Two days later the story appeared; this time the headline read: "Reed: Indians Gave Money; but Candidate Insists Casinos Not the Source."

Every few days, two new things popped up: a zit on my face and a story by Haman. It went on like this for months. Asking for a retraction, getting a yes and then a no, and then another story about the story, and then a political cartoon in the editorial section of the paper about the story in the news section. A constant stream of stories about the same thing, just with a different microscope.

Befuddled by the constant drip of inaccuracy, I once asked Ralph, "Do you think he's spiteful, or just stupid?"

"Both," said Ralph, and I think he was right. Haman wanted to make a name for himself, but wasn't savvy enough to really understand the complexity of the scandal. This resulted in story upon story, rehash after rehash, each slightly correcting or updating the last, reworking what had already been reported. The cumulative effect was to make *AJC* readers so bored and burned out on Ralph Reed, they never wanted to hear his name again. I felt their pain. But I was also about to feel a much deeper type of pain.

Lisa Baron

Our dog Jack hated the UPS guy. I mean, hated him. Schnauzy Jack (as we called him) vowed to get the UPS man and his mangy truck if it was the last thing he ever did. Our UPS man would have to stand outside the perimeter of our house (the dogs were kept in by an invisible electric fence) and throw packages as close to our doorstep as possible.

Well, it turns out that the last thing that Jack ever did, was get that dastardly truck. I was leaving the house for a quick Costco run. I was gone for one hour, maybe. When I got back, our very sweet mailman, Kirk, approached me as I got out of my car and said that he had seen a small gray dog lying in the street. "Not my Jack!" I hoped and prayed. The ironic thing was, in the years leading up to his death, I had actually run drills in my head of what I would do in the event of Jack's untimely demise. Here was my plan: Get Jimmy. There was no way I could bear to see my little Jack hurt.

Thank God, Jimmy was there that afternoon, working from his office on the third story of our Sandy Springs home. I ran upstairs and told Jimmy what Kirk the mailman had warned. The color drained from Jimmy's face. He stopped everything he was doing, flew down a flight of stairs, and charged out the front door into the street. He screamed for me to turn away. "Get back in the house, get back in the house!" But I couldn't. I watched my husband carry my limp dog's body across the yard and into the front seat of his car en route to our vet's office. As I waited for Jimmy to call me with an update, I hoped for the best, but as the minutes passed, the phone remained silent for much too long. When Jimmy called thirty minutes after being gone, I knew. Jack was gone. A piece of my heart died right along with him.

Perhaps you are wondering how we knew it was the UPS man who killed my dog. After all, we weren't there to witness the drive-by clipping of my dog's head. Four hours later, there was a UPS sticky note stuck to our front door. These words were scribbled on the Post-it that usually carries news of undelivered shoes or dresses: "Call re: your dog." When Jimmy called, the driver fessed up. Jimmy asked why it took four hours to let us know what happened to our dog and why he let a dog lie in the street to suffer. The driver said it made him uncomfortable. "Well," said Jimmy, "it made me uncomfortable having to pick my wife's dead dog up off the street."

We had Jack cremated, as Jimmy wouldn't go for taxidermy. Jack's ashes sat on our mantel in the living room, his Burberry collar hanging from the floral tin.

Fortunately (if there was anything fortunate about losing your four legged child to logistics) work kept me plenty busy.

Reporters from the *Washington Times* to the *New York Times* and *USA Today* were also showing up in Georgia to take Ralph's picture and write the campaign's obituary. *Time* magazine came in, as well as *GQ* and *Rolling Stone*, which sent a writer to one of our breakfasts. The *Rolling Stone* reporter said that our finance director, Art, a notoriously chatty man whose wife was dying of cancer, had cornered him in an attempt to block his access to the table (not true—Art just talks a lot). And he implied that Jared was gay because he was drinking a can of pink Tab. The reporter kept e-mailing me, asking about "a black church leadership program," without elaborating on what black church leadership program he was referring to, even though I kept on asking him for more information. He wrote in the story that I pointedly refused to talk about the black church issue. I knew that *Rolling Stone* was the last magazine I could expect to have any sympathy for Ralph Reed, but the story was dripping with hate, and blatant disregard for proper journalism. It was depressing, and not to mention, annoying. Even more depressing was that the evangelical newsmagazine *World* was starting to cover the scandal, too. This was not just some liberal witchhunt. The story was everywhere.

The accusations became more and more ridiculous as the campaign wore on. I got a call one day from the AP boy reporter asking me if it was true that Ralph was responsible for the rise of terrorism on the North Marianas Islands. Far-fetched, to say the least. But Ralph's veneer was cracking under the strain. I know flailing when I see flailing, and Ralph was flailing. As he spiraled, he just kept saying, "Fix this, Lisa, I need you to fix this." Seeing my friends and boss in pain was brutal. But I had to remain honest with myself about how he had gotten there. He had skated too close to the moral line he pretended to walk, and he had tripped. Nonetheless, the show still had to go on. We were still trying to run an election campaign.

He started with some image control. Ralph traded in his flashy Lexus for a Ford F150 and ditched his ostrich cowboy boots for a lower-heeled, leather look. I must tell you, I never understood the fascination with Reed's footwear. From the *New York Times* to the *Washington Post* to *GQ*—every story about Ralph on the campaign trail had some mention of his ostrich low-heeled cowboy boots. Frankly, I'm more fascinated with John Boehner's perma tan, Sarah Palin's banana clip, and I do wonder why, with all of Nancy Pelosi's money, she can't find a bra that fits. Every time I see file footage of her scampering down the congressional halls, I become uncomfortably distracted by the jiggle of her chesticles. It's no biggie if she doesn't want to wear a bra that fits—but the least she could do is walk a little slower. (Nancy, if you do want a bra that fits, there is a great store in Atlanta called Intimacy. You'll have to call and make an appointment, they book up weeks in advance.)

As the newspaper stories exploded, so did Ralph's obsessive need for control. Somehow, he still believed that if we just stuffed our prepared statement into reporters' faces, the Jack issue would just go away. The questions were always the same: Did you know? When did you know? And why did you do it? But ignoring the big white gambling elephant in the room only served to exacerbate the gaping wound. I was, as we all were, bewildered by what became Ralph's refusal to confront this nuclear-sized problem that could bring the whole campaign down if not properly contained. He seemed to be going with the Clinton "smile and wave" strategy. Every time the media asked a question about Gennifer Flowers, the model he had a sexual relationship with, Clinton would smile and wave as he was whisked off to his next event, behaving as though he had never even heard the question. Or maybe he was going with the George W. Bush "booger sugar privacy strategy," in which politicians flat-out refuse to answer questions, in order to stop the media's intrusive behavior into their lives and vices.

Ralph started to seem like a broken record, stuck in the afterglow of the rally. He was still saying things to us like, "We are going to run this race like we are seven points ahead." And I felt like saying, "You're running like we're winning, but we're not." Democrats were sniggering, saying they hoped he won the Republican nomination for lieutenant governor, because it would give their candidate a far better chance of winning in the election, so tainted was he. I wished Ralph would have been open and honest about the work he did from the beginning, and apologized. He could have told the press, "I am sorry, I didn't feel like I was being hypocritical with my work. This is what I did." Instead, he stonewalled.

When he eventually did decide to open up, it was at a Friday night event in a speech to a group of teenagers, where there was no press and where he would introduce a hundred-page briefing book on all of the policies he would introduce as lieutenant governor. He wanted us to start on it immediately, telling us, "I want this to be the most comprehensive plan ever put forth by a candidate of either party in history." Oh yeah, this oughta do the trick: a massive wad of wonk written by PhD Ralph. That should definitely turn this ship around.

After we released the policy plan, he said, we would give a speech to a teen pact, a church group of teens who were meeting on a Friday night. His speech, he said, would say that when he took the work with Jack, he made a judgment in error.

"I'll invite the media?" I said, wanting to make the best of a horrible idea.

"No," he said. "Just release the speech after I deliver my remarks."

Ralph was afraid. He knew what he had done, and so did Jack. He was trapped—if he pretended to be innocent in the press, then Jack might have retaliated in the media. If he owned up, he'd have had to publicly admit that he wasn't perfect, that he suffered from weakness and confusion, like all mortal men. In the end, the latter was too terrifying.

I confronted him.

"We're not winning, will you please stop acting like we're winning? We're losing." By this point, I knew that the gig was over. Forget the White House. Forget having Ralph as my lifelong mentor and inspiration. The future was uncertain, for all of us.

"Thank you, Lisa. I'll take that on board."

After that, he shut down. He saw that I no longer believed he was invincible. I couldn't pretend any longer that his ideas were the best, and that his strategy was solid. So he stopped talking to me.

Meanwhile, McCain's committee continued to release napalm bombs, in the form of hundreds of leaked e-mails between Ralph and Jack on our campaign, and from Jack discussing Reed.

"I need to start humping in corporate accounts!" my boss had written Abramoff in 1998.

"He is a bad version of us!" wrote Abramoff of Reed. "No more money for him." Regarding a $50,000 payment to Reed for work supporting the Choctaw, on February 7, 2002, Abramoff told his partner in crime, Scanlon, to "go ahead and pay him so I can get him off my back."

Were they really talking about the Ralph Reed I knew?

A draft engagement letter from Reed to Abramoff showed that Reed promised to "build a strong grassroots network . . . against the extension of video poker," boasting that Century Strategies had strong relationships with grassroots conservatives in Alabama, including the Alabama Christian Coalition, the Alabama Family Alliance, the Alabama Eagle Forum, the Christian Family Association, and "leading evangelical pastors such as Frank Barker of Briarwood Presbyterian Church in Birmingham. Century Strategies has on file over 3,000 pastors and 90,000 religious conservative households in Alabama that can be accessed in this effort," he said. "We can play an operational role in building a strong anti-video poker grassroots structure that will leverage the considerable contacts and reputation of our principals within Alabama, the conservative faith."

Reed asked for a $20,000 monthly retainer, concluding with, "We look forward to bringing about the desired results for you."

I still held on to the belief that maybe, just maybe, Ralph really didn't know that the money he was getting paid with was coming from the casinos. Until I read reports of an e-mail sent in April 1999 that Abramoff e-mailed Reed suggesting a direct payment to him from the Mississippi Band of Choctaw Indians, a gambling client, without moving the money through a third party first. "Any chance that a wire from Choctaw directly would be Okay?" Abramoff wrote. McCain's committee estimated that Abramoff, using casino money, paid Reed more than $4 million in three years. Like everyone else, I was learning about Ralph Reed by reading the newspapers. And I hated what I was learning.

I tried to not think about the stream of dirt that was being unearthed. Instead, Jared and I worked diligently to convince Ralph to do every television and print interview that was offered to us. We believed that in the midst of all of the chaos, Ralph's supporters should be reminded of why they fell in love with him in the first place. Our strategy was one of sunshine! But our push was met by his tug. The man who once found such pleasure in hobnobbing with reporters and was revealed in off-the-record rants, was not interested in talking to reporters anymore, insisting that either me or Jared respond ourselves or with a prepared statement. He instructed us to respond as tersely as possible. This, by the way, is Press 101 for exactly how not to handle a bad situation.

Our rapid response document, titled "Setting the Record Straight" (every campaign has a form of this to combat negative attacks or bad publicity), was not rapid or particularly responsive. What should've taken us one hour to write and distribute got caught up in editing—Ralph's editing. Sometimes our rebuttal documents took days to complete and were three pages long. Nobody reads a three-page-long press release, nobody. Not even me, and I wrote the stupid things.

There were times he was agreeable, but before he would go on-camera, a place he once considered his home away from home, I had to negotiate with the producers for what seemed like two days about what questions could and couldn't be asked—keep in mind the actual interview took about two minutes from start to finish. Reed hadn't been with the Coalition for seven years, but his work at the helm of the grassroots organization is what he is best known for. It was also what he wanted to distance himself from the furthest.

"I don't want to be identified as 'Former leader of the Christian Coalition' anymore," he continued, "and don't let them call me lobbyist, either. I'm not a lobbyist." In 2006, *lobbyist* was a another word for *crook*.

I understood why Ralph wanted to reinvent himself. I knew he wanted to leave the past in the past, ignore the ugly present, and focus on his rose-tinted version of the future. But Ralph not wanting to be known for the way he rose to power was like the late Gary Coleman not wanting to be known for *Diff'rent Strokes* and becoming unglued anytime someone said, "What you talking 'bout, Willis?"

Meanwhile, my parents had gone from Ralph's most strident opponents to his most loyal and outspoken supporters. They read every newspaper article and recorded every cable news segment devoted to the subject of Ralph Reed, and then they called to say things like, "Lisa, this is really bad," or "I don't see how you are going to win?" My dad was the one who offered strategic advice.

"Maybe Ralph should give an interview to apologize, that seems to work for every other politician," said my dad. Preaching to the choir, Dad, preaching to the choir. And my mom, well, she was upset because Abramoff was Jewish. Obsessed with Jews in the news, she becomes devastated, literally overcome with anguish, any time a Jewish person is in the newspaper or the nightly news because he/she has done something bad. Sipping her coffee (or her Pinot Noir, depending on the time of day) and shaking her head, she'll explain, "This does not make Jews look good." It was one for all and all for one in her mind, and this Jack Abramoff, in her opinion, was "reinforcing the negative stereotype people have of Jews." Right now, negative stereotyping of Jews was the last thing on my mind. I was wondering if my boss was ever going to be able to be taken seriously again.

CHAPTER 22

The Vagina Monolog

I was surprised my pussy hadn't gotten me in more trouble before now. And yes, I just said *pussy*. I was one year into leading my double life: by day, I was a Christian politician's right-hand woman; by night, a saucy *Sex and the City*-style columnist. I was married and ready to procreate. I was taking my temperature, peeing on sticks, mapping ovulation cycles, and writing about it.

Everything was going swimmingly. I was publishing right under the chinny-chin-chins of the social conservatives I served. I wrote about booze and boys and the adventures of trying to make a baby. I talked about my friends and their friends and the parties we went to, sometimes coming home at 4:00 A.M. I talked about my hot-ass hot chocolate fitness instructor, I told people about the real-life booty-shaking, rump-selling, cash- (or check-) taking hooker I saw in my California hotel lobby bar where I was staying for my cousin's wedding. It was awesome. And it was successful. Both of which surprised me. I had never had my own weekly column before, and it was a shock to me (and probably even Jimmy, although he would never admit it) that Atlantans looked forward to my 750 words every Sunday.

I was very forthright when it came to discussing my marriage—as was Jimmy on his radio show. When things were going well, I wrote about them, and when they weren't going well, I wrote about that, too. I was becoming something of a local personality, and Jimmy would sometimes invite me onto his show. (When Ari Fleischer published his book *Taking the Heat* in 2005, Jimmy double-dared me to get Ari to appear on his show. Ari had steadfastly ignored me since our little tête-à-tête in Greenville, but now that he needed to promote a book, the rules had changed. He called in to the radio station for his interview, expecting to talk to my husband about politics, not expecting to talk to me. We haven't spoken since.)

Suddenly my e-mail in-box was filling up with fan mail saying things like, "Thank you for being so honest," "I love your writing," and "I look forward to reading what you say every week." My physical mailbox was packed with VIP invitations to this party or that movie premiere. My picture was in all of the socialite magazines, and my closet was stocked with free swag. And this time, it wasn't because of who I worked for. It was because of me. I also got my fair share of hate mail, but Jimmy taught me, through example, that being in the spotlight comes with its share of aggravations. This helped to toughen my outer armor and made me a stronger person both mentally and creatively.

It was quite a contrast to what was going on at my campaign day job, where journalists were berating and dragging my boss's name through the mud. That's why I wanted to keep the momentum going. And to do this, I needed to give my people what they wanted: my crotch!

Over the Thanksgiving holiday, I told my husband Jimmy's father that I had a big pussy. Well, not in so many words. Actually I didn't use any words at all. I used a hand gesture. Unbeknownst to me, my father-in-law and Jimmy had been watching an episode of HBO's *Curb Your Enthusiasm*, which featured the creation of a hand gesture that can nonverbally indicate to a man if the woman he is with has a big vagina. This was what Jimmy told me to show to his dad. Not knowing what I was doing, I did just that. I held up the fingers of my right hand in a wide *V* shape in the direction of my father-in-law, who laughed, more than a little embarrassed.

Eventually, they explained the joke and I did think it was funny, if somewhat perturbing. That being said, if you told your father-in-law that you had a big pussy and you, in fact, did not, wouldn't you want to write 750 words to set the record straight?

The title of my December 11, 2005, column was "My Big Cavernous Pit of Love." It led in to the diatribe about my vajayjay. "Over the Thanksgiving holiday I told my father-in-law I had a big vagina," it read.

The column ran like they all did, on a Sunday. Everything seemed normal. On Monday, I went to work as usual; fought with the media as usual; read an e-mail from Big Les that was meant for someone else, as usual; drank with Mary Frances as usual. That's why it didn't even cross my mind that when the 202 exchange (the area code for Washington, DC) number appeared on my BlackBerry screen, it would be a call not only for me, but about me.

"Is this Lisa?" said the female voice on the other line.

"Yes," I said, not recognizing the female voice on the other line.

"This is Amy, and I'm with the *Washington Post*," she said.

At this point there was nothing unusual about getting a call from a reporter with the *Washington Post*.

"I write a column called 'Reliable Sources,' and I wanted to ask you about a column you wrote for, I think it's called the *Sunday Paper*?"

Motherfucker! Outed again!

"Yes," I said nervously.

"Well, it's kind of a racy thing for Ralph Reed's spokesperson to be writing. Don't ya think?"

"Yes," I said nervously.

Sensing my distress, Amy said, "Lisa, I'm not writing a gotcha item on you. At first I was going to, but then I read some of your stuff and you actually do write about working for Ralph."

With these words, the color came back into my face, and I agreed to give her an on-the-record comment, the only sensible thing I could think of at that point. Not only was Ralph going down, it seemed like I had managed to sink my own ship, all by myself. Might as well make the most of it. I forwarded Amy a publicity shot that I believed made me look the skinniest and youngest. If I had to be in the paper, I should look fabulous, right?

It was December 22, 2005, and I was on my way out west to spend the winter break with my family. I left quite early in the morning and spent four hours in an airplane. When I touched down and it was safe to turn on all electronic devices, I switched on my phone. I had twenty-five voice mails. Yes, twenty-five fucking voice mails. I heard from people I hadn't talked to in years, some whom I hadn't talked to on purpose, asking me about my vagina. Dozens of e-mails. The item had run that morning with a full-sized picture of me smiling in my tight white dress. In the top right-hand corner, was a picture of Ralph at a podium in a pose that suggested he was in the midst of delivering a fiery speech.

The headline: "Thou Shalt What?? Ralph Reed's Flack Writes a Little Blue in a Red State" led the entire column and filled the entire front section of the paper. True to her word, Amy did not write a gotcha piece.

"As Ralph Reed's longtime spokesperson, Lisa Baron has her name in the papers a lot. Her boss, the former Christian Coalition president, is running for lieutenant governor of Georgia and facing questions about his dealings with scandal-plagued lobbyist Jack Abramoff . . . But Baron is also popping up in print these days with the shockingly saucy—often downright ribald—weekly column she writes for the *Sunday Paper*, an alty sort of weekly aimed at Atlanta's young upscale types."

I called my old boss on the Whitman campaign, Jacqueline, to see what she thought of my newfound infamy. "I don't know what the big deal is," she said. "Scooter Libby wrote a book with bestiality in it, why can't you write the word *vagina*?" I think she was proud of her little cub, and was quick to mention that I had beat out Jenna Bush for the lead story. As the day went on, she would forward me write-ups of the write-up as they appeared on Wonkette.com and *National Journal*'s daily news roundup, "The Hotline." I found the story on the *Huffington Post* and *Daily Kos*. A cartoon appeared in my weekly newspaper's competitor, *Creative Loafing,* and a piece by Ralph Hallow soon followed in the *Washington Times*. The *Times* piece indicated that my risqué writings were part of a carefully orchestrated plan by me to help Ralph appeal to moderate voters. I wished I had that much control. Jaqcueline said she hoped I got fired, and if I didn't I should quit. She said that this was an opportunity for me to come out of the shadows and pursue a real writing career. I wondered if she might be right.

As the days passed, my e-mail and voice mail continued to clog with greetings and salutations from admirers and detractors alike. But there was one person suspiciously and eerily absent, someone who hadn't checked in. Did Ralph not know? Had he not seen the item? It seemed like everyone else in the world was a twitter about my twat.

On Christmas Day, to test the waters a little bit and be nice, I sent him an e-mail wishing him a great day and extending my love to him and his family. I figured if he e-mailed me back straightaway, he had not read the piece. If he ignored my electronic missive, I was fucked. He e-mailed me back, wished me a wonderful holiday break, expressed his family's love for me, and signed his name. And that was all he wrote.

Was he waiting to give me my walking papers when we got back to Atlanta? Or was I the luckiest bitch alive?

CHAPTER 23

My Burning Bush

I have a long history of making bad decisions. In middle school, I decided to streak my black hair with highlights. In high school I started smoking. And in college, in pursuit of an easy A to boost my GPA, I dropped Drugs in Society, which I knew lots about, in favor of Intro to Parenting, for which I received a C–. And now this: I write an ode to my vagina in the middle of a political campaign that is in the middle of arguably the largest lobbying scandal in modern American history.

What kind of a moron was I? After being outed by the *Washington Post* for writing about my vagina, I beat myself up in a way that suggested that I had slept through a once-in-a-lifetime Christian Louboutin sample sale or left the neighborhood bar only to learn that Robert Plant had got up and played a set with the house band ten minutes after I left. The magazine, on the other hand, was thrilled. They'd been flooded with hits, and even posted a link to the *Washington Post* story on their front page. Chat rooms of liberal websites like Huffingtonpost.com and Dailykoz.com lit up with conversations about Ralph's slutty press secretary and her article about her "big pussy" (their words, not mine). I had always known that by writing that column, I was pushing the envelope, but I hadn't thought far enough ahead to imagine anything like this happening. I worried that my mother was going to put me in the Jewish Hall of Shame, along with Jack, for my "Jews Gone Wild" antics.

Wrong again.

Both of my parents thought it was so "neat" that their daughter was prominently featured in the *Washington Post*. "Your story is at the top of the page!" my mother exclaimed. "You even beat out Jenna Bush for the top spot!" my dad gloated. My parents, who had seemingly lost all hope of their daughter ever being a respectable member of society, were now doing their best to love me for who I was—every Jewish mother's nightmare.

It had been at least a week and I still hadn't heard a peep out of Ralph on the topic. That is, until I returned back to work after the holiday break. I walked in from the parking lot and went to the twin bank of elevators. I pressed the up button and waited for my chariot to take me to the ninth floor, where I would see Mary Frances and Jared and we would Google all the coverage my clitoris had gotten over the Christmas break and laugh.

The elevator doors parted to expose an empty elevator. Empty that is except for one other passenger. Ralph. I looked at him and he looked at me. I tried not to laugh or smile because he was not laughing or smiling.

"Hi," I said like we barely knew each other.

"I take it you were busy over the holiday weekend," he said and then smiled.

"I am so sorry," I said, my voice ripe with contrition.

"Put your stuff down in your office and then come and see me. I don't want to give any more time to this than we need to, so it should only take five minutes."

Oh God, I thought. *I've finally done it. He's finally had enough of me.* I had to admit—my vagina had to be the last thing he needed to be worrying about right now. What was I thinking . . .

The elevator stopped at eight and Ralph got off. I carried on up to the ninth floor, where I got off, went to my office to plug my computer in, and then turned around to go back downstairs to meet my fate and have a sit-down with Ralph about my cooter.

I was freaking the fuck out.

"Jared, will you please come with me?" I asked our twenty-something political strategist. I felt like I needed another human in the room whom I could ask at random points during the day, week, and pretty much the rest of my life, "Did I really just sit down with the former head of the Christian Coalition to talk about my bearded clam?" and then Jared could confirm that, "Yes, it actually did happen."

On the way up to Ralph's office, Jared told me about a conversation he had the previous night at a fund-raiser with Rebecca "I don't talk to my daughter because she is a lesbian" Street. Apparently, Rebecca had pulled him aside at the get-together featuring Mississippi Governor Haley Barbour and said that she had been forwarded my column from a reporter. She had read it and came to the conclusion that I was a pornographer and I needed to be fired. Apparently, my pussy piece was interfering with her ability to witness to voters about Jesus Christ and Ralph's campaign. My onetime BFF who had greeted me with a hello and a kiss had now turned into a big C U Next Tuesday.

Jared and I walked into Ralph's office and took seats next to each other on the couch. Ralph finished typing out an e-mail, hit SEND, and then took his seat in the wing back chair that no one ever sat in but him. He looked at me and I looked at him and then in an effort to be done with this conversation as soon as possible, I started talking, and not bull-shitting.

I opened with telling him that despite all indications, I was not stupid. I had been writing my column for some time now, it had been gaining in popularity, and I wanted it to continue to gain in popularity. That's why I made the decision to write about my conversation with my father-in-law. I pointed out that there were many, many words I could've used to describe my nether regions, but after much consideration, I stuck with the biological term. As a woman who understands the power of words, I used the word that I remembered being broadcast in my sixth-grade health class. I presented my case in such a way that I did not have to actually say the word *vagina* to Ralph, and focused instead on explaining the thought process behind my choice to broadcast the diatribe about my beaver.

Then Ralph spoke, expressing disappointment in my actions. As he did, I looked over his shoulder at the large unframed window and fantasized about jumping out. Remember the famous scene in *When Harry Met Sally*, when Billy Crystal's character, Harry Burns, and Meg Ryan's character, Sally Albright, are shopping in Sharper Image? Harry begins testing out the karaoke machine by singing "Surrey with the Fringe on Top" from the classic musical, *Oklahoma*. Harry, dumped by his wife for a bald tax attorney the year before, launches into a dance and a song to the well-loved show tune from the 1943 Rodgers and Hammerstein classic. It's a playful moment of silliness, that he would've loved to have kept between Meg, himself, and a store of faces he never met. Halfway through the chorus, Harry looks up and recognizes two faces: his ex-wife and her new fiancé, Ira. He realizes that just six years earlier he was happy and he was in love. And, as he puts it (or as award-winning screenwriter Nora Ephron put it), ". . . six years later you find yourself singing 'Surrey with The Fringe on Top,' in front of Ira."

I was having my "Surrey with the Fringe on Top" moment. Six years earlier, Ralph and I were in professional love and on our way to happily ever after. Today I got caught, singing "Surrey with the Fringe on Top," in front of Ralph. Only I wasn't riding a surrey, I was writing a column and the fringe was the colorful language I used to describe what had happened to me and my poodle that fateful Father's Day. The feeling was one of utter humiliation.

"We don't need this in the campaign," he said. "Rebecca is up in arms and has asked me to fire you." His words hung in the air like a stale fart. So, I had upset the Christians. I felt my sheepishness morph into indignation. I recalled how whenever the chips were down for Ralph, I had run to those Christians' homes and defended him. "I know what's in his heart," I would tell them about Ralph and why they should forgive him for past actions. "He's a better person because of this," I said. "He's closer to Christ," I assured them. Now they were after me. These men and women whom I had fought with had turned sides on me the minute I stopped behaving the way they thought I should behave. Now I had a bunch of holy-rollers heading after me with pitchforks. Question was— what was worse, talking about vaginas, or profiteering from Indian tribes with Jack Abramoff? Faced with that question, I gained some clarity.

I made a pact with myself. If Ralph wanted to fire me, so be it. If he wanted to keep me on staff, but asked me to stop writing my column: no way. My bush, not Ralph, was the gift that kept on giving. As had happened to Moses so many thousands of years ago, my burning bush had spoken to me, and it said: pave your own way, and stand your ground.

Ralph did not want me fired. And the truth is, I was thankful. It would have been traumatizing for me to leave. I wanted to finish what I had started.

But Ralph did ask me to write an apology letter to Street. Surprising myself a little, I refused. Flat-out refused. To me, Rebecca Street is a despicable person with a black heart. If anybody should be writing an apology letter, it should be Rebecca to her daughter whom she won't speak to because she identifies sexually and emotionally with another woman. Who casts out a child like that? An innocent child whom God made exactly the way she is meant to be: perfect.

The meeting ended with me agreeing to think about penning an apologetic paragraph, not to Rebecca, but to whomever it might concern. As Jared and I left Ralph's office, something caught my eye. Sitting in a fanned-out pile on a round desk in Ralph's office was a stack of brochures with information about the Guardasil vaccine. At the time, the product was just coming to market, and I can only assume, having never actually been told what the scope of the work was or if he even did any work for the company's manufacturer, that Ralph might have been hired to cool the jets of the Christian set who believed the vaccine to protect young girls from contracting the human papillomavirus (HPV) was just another way to increase promiscuity. If they got the vaccine on time, they wouldn't think twice about accepting a hot beef injection.

I approached the table to get a closer look, and picked up the brochure. "So you can talk about genital warts, but I can't say the word *vagina?*"

And with that I turned around, walked out the door, and got back to work.

Chapter 24

Still Crazy
After All These Years

Deep down, deep down, in a place that was even hard for me to find, I was sorry for the commotion I had caused. But I wasn't sorry that I had taken one giant step out of Ralph's shadow and into my own light. I battled with Ralph over the apology letter issue. So he wrote a letter of apology to Rebecca himself. He then asked that I stop writing the column. I didn't stop writing my column. I had hoped I had heard the last of it. I was speeding up the interstate praying that the Washington, DC, pollster the campaign had finally hired didn't know about my whisker biscuit flap. I probably should have worn something more nun-like to throw him off of the scent of Crotch Gate, but I was late and the only thing I could find in my closet that was clean was a clingy black crepe minidress. I hoped he wouldn't take one look at me and wonder if the reason Ralph's campaign was tanking was a result of my undeniable whorishness.

The meeting was a presentation of a five-day statewide poll the campaign had commissioned. Campaign-commissioned polls are always the most insightful, the most accurate, and the least flattering. That's because we bring our own skeletons out of the closet for the purpose of testing just how nuclear a spotty past could become if introduced by an opponent. An example of this might be, "Would you still vote for George W. Bush if you knew that he had been arrested for a DUI?" The voter will either tell you that there is no way in hell they'd want a former juvenile offender for president or they'll tell you that, yes, they would vote for a former kid criminal, but only if the candidate talked about the arrest before it was released publicly and explained what happened. It was obvious to political hacks everywhere that when the Democrats released the Bush's drunk driving arrest to the media, who, in turn, put it out there for public consumption, it tested high in the unfavorable column for George W. Bush. That's why the Gore campaign (presumably) released the arrest literally days before the 2000 election.

Today's closed-door round table was the tactical tool we needed to get a complete snapshot of how the campaign was faring statewide. The findings would reveal our strengths and weaknesses; i.e., how deadly had the Jack Abramoff scandal been to our campaign? We all pretty much knew that we were DOA, but there's nothing quite like empirical data to really drive the point home.

In the first six months of the campaign, our political director quit and we were never able to find a replacement. I think at one point we were offering $75,000 to anyone who would come to Georgia to take political director. We ended up promoting from within and appointed a boy who was underqualified and perpetually overdressed. To put this in perspective, when accepting my job, I took one for the team and agreed to making $1,500 a month in the primary. We agreed I would get a pay raise and a bonus for the general election. On top of that, we solicited dozens and dozens of media consultants and pollsters until one finally, out of obligation to past referrals, obliged. Look, these guys love money. And what they love as much as money is power. And the only thing they love, as much as both of them combined, is being a panelist on CNN. Fuck the train, if any of these flies thought Ralph could win, they'd hop a midnight *plane* to Georgia!

Plus, how could days upon days of front-page stories in the Atlanta paper go unnoticed by voters? At some point, even if they thought that Ralph was the target of a smear campaign, they would grow tired of reading about him. That said, I hoped I was wrong, we all hoped we were wrong. I hoped that we were still running a viable campaign, that when the votes were cast we would prevail, making us all heroes, and Ralph lieutenant governor of Georgia. We all did. Especially Ralph, who had personally dumped hundreds of thousands of his own money into the campaign coffers.

I was running about fifteen minutes late, yet I made the decision that it was far more important I have my nonfat one-Equal double latté for the meeting than sit there, accepting that the DC based pollster was judging me.

Once I got to the Duluth office park, I screeched into the parking lot, muttering obscenities at the smokers on their smoke breaks who congregated just off the sidewalks of the office park and on the street. I parked my Jeep Liberty, smiled pleasantly at the women who continued to pull on their cancer sticks, and sprinted toward the elevator. I took it up to the ninth floor and hightailed to the campaign office.

"Hey, Lisa," Intern Jeff said flatly from behind the 1999 PC the campaign used to update addresses and phone numbers. He looked like he hadn't slept in days.

"Hey. Glad to see you back, are you feeling better?" I queried.

"Yeah."

"You know, you get sick more than any other college sophomore I have ever met. You must've caught the H1N1 strain of the cocktail flu this time."

"Ha, ha," he said, not laughing. "Hey, Lisa, come here," he said, catching me right before I opened the conference room door. "You didn't hear this from me, but Ralph saw the board in your office and he told Jared to tell you to take it down.

"Also . . ." Intern Jeff continued.

"Seriously, Intern Jeff, I love you, but I'm already late," I said with papers and notepads falling out of my arms.

"Tom Edsall of the *Washington Post* called for you. Isn't that the old dude who gave us $10 for a Reed for Lt. Governor T-shirt and then told you that you should be writing for *Playgirl*?" he asked.

"Yes. That's the one . . . can you send his info to my BlackBerry, pretty please?"

I shoved my belongings under my left arm and swung open the door with my right. The door was heavier than I remembered. Thankfully my two-inch black patent heel stopped the door from smacking me in the face. I squeezed my body through the crack I had saved in the door and it snapped behind me, shutting out any other light than the glow from the PowerPoint presentation.

I set my Starbucks down on the oval-shaped conference table, winked at Jared, and took a seat, tugging on the hem of my skirt, trying to make it longer. I stared intently up at the screen as we went through the polling data, trying not to look at Ralph, a rivulet of perspiration trickling down the backs of my thighs.

Ralph was seated across the table from us, his BlackBerry and bottled designer water resting on the table in front of him. While Ralph stared at the presentation, I stared at him. His green Ted Baker oxford hung lazily off his upper body and the hue of his skin gave away yet another golf game. He pulled a swill of water from the bottle and continued to listen.

"Republican voters want more military spending, and the northern suburbs want nothing to do with the city of Atlanta, they want to be their own identity," the pollster explained matter-of-factly, continuing, "They want better schools, better jobs, and typical bread-and-butter Republican issues."

But Ralph wasn't paying for a big-shot Washington, DC, pollster to come to Georgia so he could tell us that Republican ideals are alive and well in the South. He paid him to learn what was contained in slides ten through fifteen—if the Jack Abramoff scandal would bring down his entire political grassroots empire, an empire he built from the ground up over twenty years ago specifically to elect him to statewide office, and beyond.

"This," the pollster said, pointing to an upward arrow on the screen, "is when we asked people how they viewed Ralph, and we only mentioned his position as the former executive director of the Christian Coalition. As you can see they respond favorably."

The next tap of his index finger, though, which revealed the next slide, was like unzipping the body bag so the family could identify the body. "This," he said, pointing to a steadily declining red line, "is when we mentioned Ralph's name along with Jack Abramoff's. Over 60 percent of the Republicans most likely to vote in the primary were aware of Ralph's involvement in the Abramoff lobbying scandal." The graphic wasn't pretty. The slow drip of press stories and leaked e-mails between Jack and Ralph were taking a toll. The corpse had been identified, and its name was Ralph.

LIFE OF THE PARTY

Some might consider it strange that voters could have a favorable opinion of Ralph as the former executive director of the Christian Coalition, and then in the next breath—when asked about his involvement in the Abramoff scandal—would say they wouldn't vote for him to be Georgia's next lieutenant governor.

But in the civic soul of every Republican, or really any voter, lies the suspicion that politicians who shout from the tops of soap boxes plastered with Bible passages are either full of shit, hiding something, or gay. And, quite frankly, who can blame them?

After Jim Bakker got caught with one hand in the cookie jar and the other in his secretary's pants; and Ted Haggard, who led the fight against gay marriage, was caught paying a prostitute—and one with a penis, no less—modern voters were suspicious of Bible-waving public figures. Republicans were in trouble. They had scandal fatigue, lumped together with an ideology that no longer, solely on its own (pro-life, anti-gay, anti-stem cell research), appealed to a changing electorate. It was the New Millennium, baby, and the Cleavers had gone wind and solar, or at a minimum they were open to considering the idea of global warming without dismissing it as an anti-business concept propagated by long-haired hippie liberals. Election by election, the Republicans were dwindling in numbers, and in another cycle they would be down to nothing more than their social conservative base.

"It's killing me!" Ralph exclaimed. "Look at that, I'm taking bullets to the chest!"

We all sat quietly, especially me, who, like a dutiful office wife, just smiled and nodded, trying to look hopeful. "I'm on trial here because of leaked e-mails and business I did with Jack six years ago? This is insane!" He was getting worked up. "If John McCain thinks I did a number on him in South Carolina, he hasn't seen anything yet!" Jared and I looked at each other like children who finally understand what their parents were saying when they started spelling out words like *S-E-X* or *D-I-V-O-R-C-E*. "I don't want to know. I don't know!" I shouted, looking to Jared, who soon joined in the chant, both of us covering our ears and shaking our heads like toddlers having a temper tantrum.

"He hates our party, you know," Ralph said, looking squarely at me like I was some sort of John McCain apologist, just because I was pro-cocktails and pro-choice. "That presidential wannabe will not get in here and try to divert our campaign and take us off our message!" I'd never seen him this angry.

Ralph instructed the pollster to go back to the slide that showed us winning if the campaign was waged on the following mantra: Ralph Reed of the Christian Coalition. "See, right there," he exclaimed, "that's what we need to be doing. We gotta get out there and remind them of who I am, and why they like me." The boom of his voice and the conviction in his words had that familiar hypnotic effect, like a Jedi mind trick: it made us believe that the three of us sitting in that dark conference room in a tiny suburb in Georgia could not only win this campaign, we could take on the world. Classic Ralph: you start a meeting hanging off the window ledge and you end it feeling invincible.

And just like that, our campaign reversed course. We went from a mainstream, balanced-budget, tax-cutting, pro-family candidate who espoused big ideas such as the Taxpayer Dividend Act, Youth Challenge Academies, and groundbreaking transportation systems, back to square one: hawking dogma.

Maybe he was right.

After all, he chaired the Georgia Republican Party in 2002, helped elect Saxby Chambliss to the U.S. Senate and Sonny Perdue as the first GOP governor in 130 years, gained control of the state senate for first time since Reconstruction, spearheaded the successful legal challenge of legislative maps that paved the way for the General Assembly GOP majority—and there was that Christian Coalition experience where he helped elect the first Republican Congress in forty years. He was the Jesus of the GOP. On second thought, he was more like Moses: a man who led his people to the Promised Land but was never allowed to go in himself.

I left the conference room, went straight into my office, and erased John McCain's name from the "on notice" column. He was now "dead to me."

CHAPTER 25

Good Night and Good Luck

Debate prep with Ralph was always strangely satisfying. Jared and I would grill Ralph as if we were journalists chosen as moderators for the lieutenant governor debates, and I got to ask pointed questions like, "Where did you think the money was coming from?" and "Was there any attempt to obscure the source of the funds by running it through nonprofits?" I asked these questions sipping my unsweetened tea, while pretending to be a debate panelist and deep down wondering what the truth was. Ralph was in no way offended by my aggressive line of questioning, because he suspected he would be getting these same questions from actual journalists. Which he did.

The first two debates were all about Jack. What Ralph thought about Jack, what our opponent thought about Jack. And then things changed. When it was clear that there was no more anyone could say about Jack

Abramoff, the topic went to actual policy discussions on how these men—Ralph and his opponent, Casey Cagle—sought to make Georgia better. Ralph dazzled the journalist panel as well as the voters who bothered to watch the publicly broadcasted debates, with his deep and broad knowledge of public policy. Our opponent didn't have much to offer in the way of thought leadership. The election was more a referendum on Ralph. Do we trust this guy, or don't we?

It was a typically sticky Georgia July, and with four days left to go until Election Day, the editors and journalists of the *AJC* were hot for Ralph Reed, having written more than a hundred stories about him in the run-up (this number does not include blogs about Ralph or political cartoons featuring Ralph). The stories included a comprehensive look at his past corporate work, political work, and opinion about which way he had wiped his ass over the last ten years. The paper published less than five stories about our opponent, one of the stories being a side-by-side table of biographical information of every candidate running for office in Georgia.

I confronted Haman—why the lopsided coverage? The first response was, "We will write about the other guy later." There were four days left before the voters went to the polls, so I very much doubted it. His second answer was a little more believable: "We expect Ralph to win, because the other guy is an unknown." The truth was, the daily bullets to the chest weren't so much about Ralph being a tangential figure in a headline-grabbing lobbying scheme. It was because Haman, like a lot of people, wanted Ralph kicked off his moral high horse. And this was the opportunity they had been hoping for. Ralph, being as smart as he is, should've known that this would happen and should've refused the work in the first place.

Then a funny thing happened on the way to Election Day. The polls started to take a turn. Some polling numbers even had our campaign up seven to eight points. My head was spinning.

"We're going to win the nomination," Mary Frances said, sitting in my office eating cookies. "I just know it. You want to go to Mexico before the general election?"

"Fuck, yeah!" I said. "Do you think, even though I am thirty-four, I can still wear a bikini? Is there an age cut-off?" I wondered out loud.

"Lisa, you got some tits in there that are dying to say *hola* to some islanders," she said. "And P.S.: There's no age cut-off. Hello, Pamela Anderson."

"I'm not exactly Pamela Anderson," I said.

"No, but you aren't Kirstie Alley, either."

My BlackBerry began to vibrate, knocking over my framed photo of Steven Colbert. "RR Home," the screen read. We had been hit with a lawsuit from an Indian tribe out in Texas. We were back on the front cover of every local and national newspaper . . . again. My mom called to say that she was proud of me and loved me, although this time, she admitted it really wasn't looking very good for the Reed campaign. Even Jared, my solid, unflappable Jared, was wringing his hands nervously. As I sat in my office squaring off with reporters once more, my heart sank as I listened to the volunteer kids out in the hall, calling voters in support of Ralph in the final days leading up to the election.

"Oh yes, sir," they would say, "I'm sure good will prevail over evil."

July 18, 2006: It was election night, and we were holed up at the Buckhead Intercontinental Hotel in Ralph's suite, waiting for the numbers to roll in. It was me, Ralph and JoAnne, Jared, Tim, and for some reason, Catholic Deal Hudson, who still owes me money for buying his drinks on election night 2000 in Austin, Texas. We were all looking at our watches and making nervous small talk. I prayed to the sweet Baby Jesus, Mary Magdalene, and all the Christian saints I could think of (sorry, God, but yes, I did) to be kind to Ralph.

Ralph received a call on his cell. After hanging up, he looked at me and smiled.

"Lisa, I am going to print off my speech. Will you go pick it up from the printer in the lobby?"

He had prepared two speeches, a victory speech and a concession speech. I went downstairs to the front desk and waited for the pages to feed out from the printer. It was his concession speech. The Republican primary voters of Georgia had soundly rejected a Reed candidacy. They didn't do it because he wasn't smart or didn't have better ideas. They did it because they were tired of the scandal. They were tired of us. We lost 44 percent to 56 percent. A twelve-point landslide in a primary against a nobody. This was a failure of biblical proportions.

I met him downstairs in the hotel party room, which was pretty vacant. People smell a loser, and they don't want to stick around. I got the press ready and told them Ralph was going to be making a concession speech. Haman was there, and one of Ralph's supporters yelled at him, "You're an asshole, Haman!" Our nice finance director was so distraught, he yelled at a news anchor, "It was the media's fault!" I couldn't take my eyes off Haman. He looked back at me, eyes gleaming and said, "You know, I would never write disparaging things about someone who was going through a terrible situation."

"Just leave him alone, Haman," I said and walked away, disgusted.

I watched Ralph give his concession speech, his wife and four kids by his side. I felt like I was watching someone read their own obituary.

"Tonight my candidacy for lieutenant governor comes to an end," he said. "But the ideas for which I stood, the values for which you have fought, and the governing philosophy that we believe in will go on, and it will go on to victory."

It was all over now. At least for me it was. Ralph knew it—maybe that's why he didn't thank me in his speech, even though I had been on his campaign staff longer than anyone else. It was okay. I had made my peace with it.

The morning after, I called Ralph from my bed. I was exhausted. While I waited for him to answer the phone, I couldn't help but wonder if I would've tried harder or spoken up more often or didn't write about my "down there," maybe the outcome might have been different. Of course not, I remembered. Ralph lost because he put money before morals.

"Lisa," he said quietly into the phone. "I'm sorry. I'm sorry I put you through this, I'm sorry I put my family through this."

I couldn't let him finish what he was saying. I could handle the lectures and the pontificating and even the occasional silent treatments. I could take the talking down to and the quick-tongued retorts he used to call my judgment into question; I could even handle his use of the term *genital warts* in a closed-door meeting. But I just couldn't handle hearing Ralph Reed throw himself off the pedestal I had spent so many years building for him.

I interrupted.

"I just want you to know that if I had the chance to do this entire campaign all over again . . . knowing everything I know—even knowing that it would have the same outcome, I would do it, no question," I said, my voice breaking up. "Everything in life that's important hasn't been touched. You have a beautiful wife and four gorgeous, healthy children who love you. You know, I always tell my family that everything I have that's good, I got as a result of coming to work for you, Ralph. For now, this is how our lives are meant to be."

"Thank you, Lisa. I am also sorry I set you up with Jason. I truly had no idea."

I believe in fate. If the governor of Arizona hadn't been indicted on federal fraud charges, I would never have moved to Washington, DC. If Bob Dole would've become president of the United States, I wouldn't have worked for Governor Christie Whitman. If Christie Whitman would've been nice, I wouldn't have found myself wasting away in Tallahassee. And if Tallahassee would've been a rewarding experience both personally and professionally instead of the cesspool of misfortune that it was, I would have never, ever in one million years gone to work for Ralph Reed. And if I never went to work for Ralph Reed, I might have wound up working in Washington, DC, wearing bad blue skirt suits and sensible shoes. And if I had never written about my "cavernous pit of love," I would've never gotten the call from the *Washington Post*, and if that call never happened and the subsequent media attention that resulted, I would never have found my own voice, this book, and my own path in life.

A couple of weeks after the campaign ended, I realized that I had lived through something really remarkable. Remarkably bad, in so many ways, but remarkable nonetheless. I started writing straightaway, penning the outline that grew into this book. Then, a miracle—I discovered that I was pregnant. My sister-in-law had told me that I needed to put some weight on if I was going to get pregnant. But with all the stress relating to the campaign, I had no appetite. I had gone so far as to schedule an appointment with my OB/GYN, so worried was I about my fertility. The doctor gave me a pep talk and a pack of Clomid, and I was set to take the fertility drug. But I never did need to take Clomid—after Ralph's failed bid for lieutenant governor, and while on vacation with Jimmy in the Galapagos Islands, I got pregnant. My son, Micah, whom I named after my biological father, had wisely opted to wait for the chaos to subside before coming along.

The saddest consequence of the whole saga, for me, was saying good-bye to Big Les and the girls. This time, I think we all knew it really was the end of an era. But we were happy in the knowledge that we had spent some of the best years of our lives together. As my belly grew, and I shared the stories of my pregnancy with my friends, family, and readers, I thanked Ralph for unintentionally enabling me to find my path as a writer. And I wondered what the future held—for both of us.

If I know Ralph, I thought, *he won't be gone for long.*

EPILOGUE

A manda married and has a little baby girl whom she dressed up like Madonna for Halloween.

Emily is married, living in the suburbs with three little boys under the age of three.

Mary Frances went to work for John McCain on his presidential campaign.

Jared got married to the beautiful Jenn, and is now a big-shot political consultant who makes a lot of money (and if he doesn't, he should).

United States Senator John McCain became the Republican nominee for president of the United States. When he needed the help of the conservative wing of the party he tried to destroy, he didn't have it and put Alaska Governor Sarah Palin on the ticket with him. Oh, and when he held a fund-raiser in Georgia, his wife, Cindy, sent word that Ralph Reed was not welcome.

Lisa Baron

Ralph wrote a best-selling book on the subject of presidential politics. One of the main characters, "Lisa," is the fictional communications director to the evangelical protagonist. After spending three years out of the public eye, he launched his Faith and Freedom Coalition in 2009, marking his official return to the national political arena. The Evangelical and Tea Party movements, he said, are "inextricably intertwined."

Big Les, well, in the event of her untimely demise, she has instructed Amanda to enter her home and remove the Jack Rabbit from her closet.

John Haman, well, who cares.

And me? I wrote a book, had a baby, and sadly, Jimmy and I divorced in 2010. As much as we loved each other, love did not conquer all. But life has its way and its rhythm, and in 2011 I married the man I will spend the rest of my life with, Sheldon, a doctor (a nephrologist, to be precise) with long rock 'n' roll hair. I stopped searching for coattails to cling on to, and I've given up looking for knights in shining armor. I stand in front of, not behind, the curtain, and if I fail or succeed, it is as a result of my own decisions. Yes, it's more work, more risk, and causes a lot more headaches, but guess what—I couldn't be happier.

ACKNOWLEDGMENTS

This book, and for that matter, my career (and life) would not have been possible without the love, help, and advice of some truly incredible people I met along the way. To all of you, I say: thank you for taking a chance on me by including me on your team, in your lives, and in some cases, into your families.

All men might be created equal, but all agents are not. My agent, Jamie Brenner, is not just a kick-ass agent who believed in me from day one, she is also a great friend, a kindred spirit, and a woman who truly espouses the essence of this book: self-reliance. To the handsome and talented Adam Chromy: thank you for seconding my motion not to name this book "Teabagger." Thank you to Julie Doughty and Caroline Ryder for your talents and discipline. Thank you to the entire Kensington team for believing in me, with special accolades and love to Michaela Hamilton and Amy Pyle for never, ever giving up on this first-time writer.

To my first boss, Governor Fife Symington's Press Secretary Doug Cole: Doug, had it not been for you, my political career would've ended before it even got started, as was suggested by the memo written to you by my then immediate supervisor who asked you to fire me. Doug, you showed me the ropes, and through watching you, I learned the craft of being a political communications professional. I love you, Doug, and I'm sorry for always barging into your office when you were on the phone with the press.

ACKNOWLEDGMENTS

Bettina Celaya Nava, Kim Grace Sabo and Trisha Reynolds: I can do nothing but smile and laugh (and laugh, and laugh) when I think about you three girls. I love you more than I can ever express. And Bettina, if you would've had me, I would've turned for you. Love, Alanis.

Steve Kupka, I will never forget the day when you and I sat down in the candidate's apartment and I looked at you and said, "You realize that you and I are responsible for creating public policy for the state of Iowa." In hindsight, it's probably a good thing we lost. But I walked away from that campaign a winner, because I found in you and your beautiful wife, Susie, lifelong friends. Your children are beautiful, and I love being in the company of the Kupkas.

David Israelite, without you, there would really be no book, because there would've been no job with Ralph Reed. David, when you called me to tell me about the communications director's job available in Ralph's Atlanta office, you threw me a life raft. In Atlanta, I found myself, my voice, gave birth to my son, and met the man of my dreams. I repaid you a few years back, when I introduced you to one of my hottest girlfriends. I considered that my way of saying thank you. But I hope this works, too.

Amanda, Emily, and my beloved Big Les: It was, I believe, nothing short of divine providence that put us all on the ninth floor of a half-occupied office building in a then-underdeveloped suburb in Georgia working for Ralph Reed. (I can hear Freakazoid screeching his first and last name right now!) It was the perfect configuration and it remains one of the best times of my life, and you women are among the loves of my life. Big Les, you are one of the most incredible women and mothers I have known. You are loyal, honest, loving, and tolerant. You deserve only the best, and I consider it my personal quest to shine a light on a woman who has spent much of her life in the background. I love you.

Jared and his beautiful wife, Jenn, the real Mary Frances (you know who you are), and Josh: Come on, that was fun! I love all of you very much, and I treasure the continued happy hours and times we spend together. I look forward to continuing down our path of a lifetime of friendship.

Ralph, you are perhaps the one I should thank the most. Because of you, I found my voice. When people ask me if you will be mad about the book, I smile and say, "I assure you, Ralph Reed has faced greater battles and more unusual obstacles than his previous aide writing a book about throwing up on Wayne Newton and writing a column about her vagina."

To my beautiful and elegant grandmother, Sylvia Gimbel, you are a role model and one of the most important women in my life. I love you so much.

To Ellen Woodard, Juli Silver, Jessica Dauler, Tara Friedman (and Demi), Mary Simon, Rev Jain, Stephanie Toettcher, Rebecca Miller, Lara Evans, Jason Miller, Stephanie Gimbel, Jenny Rider, Alan Judd (one of the good ones), Amy Argetsinger, Patrick Best, Conal Byrne, Jack and Frances Shore, Ginger Emas, Jonathan and Michelle Lerner, and the exquisite Sally Koslow: Your collective love, support, and humor have been and remain immeasurable.

Chris Bird, thank you for telling me I am "vivacious" as opposed to "loud," and to my dear Dana Sandweiss Friedman for everything. To Corey Waller for always believing in me and helping me to believe that I could "live the life I imagined."

Daniella, where to begin? You are my confidante, my conscience, my editor, my therapist, my stylist, my photographer, my voice of reason, and my precious son's godmother. You bring me to my knees with laughter, to tears with gratitude, and there were some days, when life got too heavy, that you were my oxygen. Everyone deserves to have a friend like you.

ACKNOWLEDGMENTS

Serge, you are my cheerleader, my pal, and one of the best people I know. Now, get that tux all shined up—we've got some parties to go to.

To my parents—this book is for you because you have been there for me, always. I am who I am today because you taught me to be strong, fearless, and self-assured. I can only hope that I am half the parent to my kids as you have been to me. I've hit a couple of bumps along the road of life. When this happened, family and friends frequently remarked how impressed and proud of me they were for being so strong. The reason I could be so strong is because I have you. You always, always, had my back, and I love you.

To my brother Scott: Thank you for opening the Johnny Law Wellness Center and maintaining it even during the off-season. You are an incredible person and brother, and your unconditional love, complete acceptance, and unique understanding of who I am means more to me than you will ever know. But hopefully now you know, because I just wrote it in my book. To Robyn, who can, if you wanted, exact revenge on me for the rest of your life, you are an incredible support system and champion. Your unwavering loyalty and interest in my life (including forwarding my writing around to everyone) makes me feel very happy. I will try to be a phone person. To the fabulous Sari and Mark, I love you very much and consider coming from a family of five something to brag about. To Candice and Ian, I love you. Ian, your enthusiasm for me and my work (from the get-go!) is something I truly treasure, and Candice, thank you for your everlasting friendship and support.

Sheldon, if I had to create the perfect man to write into the story of my life, he would be you. You are a kind, generous, and wonderful man who shows me love, acceptance, compassion, and partnership every day. You take my breath away. Every day I fall more and more in love with you.

Micah, my beautiful son, my love for you knows no bounds. You are

ACKNOWLEDGMENTS

the apple of my eye, the sunshine of my life, and the best thing that has ever happened to me. When you grow up (like, really up, maybe in your twenties?), I want you to read this book between the lines. And when you do, please follow its heart. My sweet child, I pray you, too, follow your dreams, pursue your passions, listen to your heart in consultation with your head, and never be afraid to fail. And on those occasions when you do find yourself afraid, intimidated, or unsure, I've got your back. Always.

Finally, I'd like to thank red wine, Xanax, and Bruce Springsteen: without this triple threat, this book would never have gotten written.